GRAMERCY NEIGHBORHOOD ASSOCIATES, INC.

P.O. Box 678 · Madison Square Station · New York, NY 10159

NO. 60 GRAMERCY PARK NORTH - EMERY ROTH, ARCHITECT
Water-tower pavilion and penthouses, looking northeast
(See pages 22-23)

GRAMERCY
ITS ARCHITECTURAL SURROUNDINGS

Preserving the Neighborhood's
Important Contributing Buildings

Introduction and Text by
ANDREW SCOTT DOLKART

Preface by
BRENDAN GILL

Foreword by
STEPHEN GARMEY

GRAMERCY NEIGHBORHOOD ASSOCIATES, INC.
Historic Preservation Committee

GRAMERCY NEIGHBORHOOD ASSOCIATES, INC.

Library of Congress Catalog Card Number 96-75682
Gramercy Neighborhood Associates, Inc.
**Gramercy, Its Architectural Surroundings: Preserving the
Neighborhood's Important Contributing Buildings**

ISBN 0-9651763-0-4

First Edition

Printed in Hong Kong

**Published by Gramercy Neighborhood Associates, Inc., P. O. Box 678,
Madison Square Station, New York, NY 10159.**

GRAMERCY
ITS ARCHITECTURAL SURROUNDINGS

PART I: PROPOSED GRAMERCY PARK HISTORIC DISTRICT EXTENSION

PART II: PROPOSED 17TH STREET/IRVING PLACE HISTORIC DISTRICT

PART III: PROPOSED INDIVIDUAL LANDMARK BUILDINGS

GRAMERCY AREA
HISTORIC PRESERVATION STUDY

- **EXISTING DISTRICT** (DESIGNATED 1966)
- **HISTORIC DISTRICT EXTENSION** (DESIGNATED 1988)
- **PROPOSED EXTENSION**
- **PROPOSED NEW DISTRICT**
- **PROPOSED INDIVIDUAL LANDMARK**
- **EXISTING INDIVIDUAL LANDMARK**

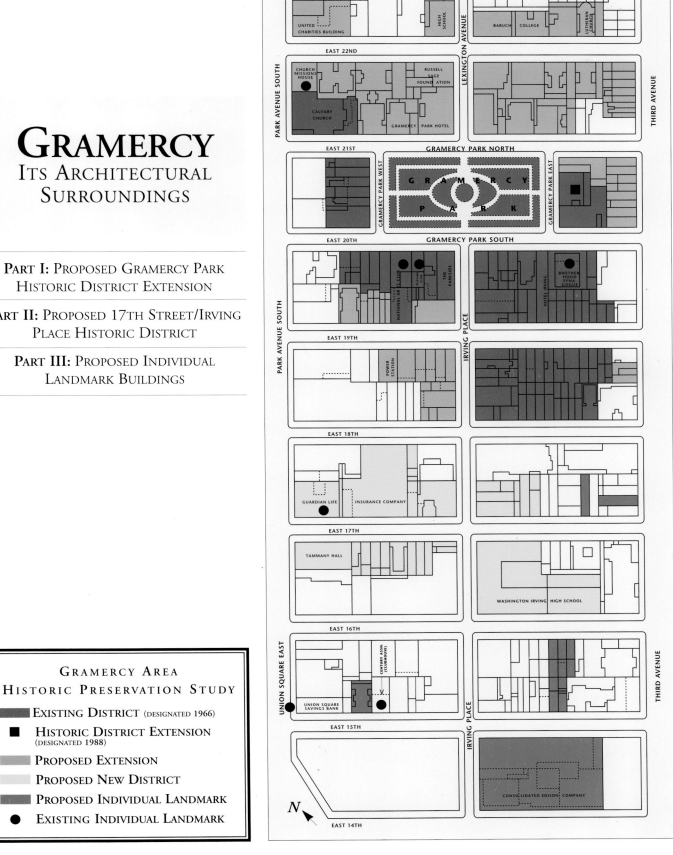

No. 121 East 17th Street
A former carriage house erected c. 1854 (See pages 68-69)

NO. 81 IRVING PLACE
Terra-cotta detail
(See pages 58-59)

T HE GRAMERCY PARK HISTORIC DISTRICT was designated in the infancy of the Landmarks Preservation Commission, almost 30 years ago, and has since often been cited as a model of its kind. For over a hundred and fifty years the little park has served as the heart of what is truly a neighborhood, much cherished by residents of its rowhouses and apartment houses and by the occupants of commercial buildings as well. Though the park cannot be expanded, the historic district assuredly can be and ought to be, reinforcing within its new boundaries that sense of "belonging" which is indispensable to urban preservation. We have learned much over the years about the economic value of designating whole districts rather than individual structures; we have learned still more about the degree to which living in a historic district awakens a shared interest in the history of the area and in the maintenance of its appearance and amenities. Given that the initial designation of the district, in 1966, reflected the caution of a commission not yet certain of how far it might go, the expansion of the historic district that is being proposed by the Gramercy Neighborhood Associates, Inc., strikes me as modest. The city has everything to gain by its adoption.

T HE GRAMERCY PARK HISTORIC DISTRICT has too often been thought to be simply a collection of 19th-century houses surrounding a private park. In reality, it is part of a rich urban mixture of townhouses, apartment, commercial, and institutional buildings, and great old trees, all reinforcing each other. It is therefore now being proposed that the original district be extended to include more of this vital context.

It should be recalled that when the Gramercy Park Historic District was designated in 1966, the Landmarks Preservation Commission had been in existence barely a year. The Designation Report is only five pages long, as compared with the 21 required for the addition of a single building, 36 Gramercy Park East, in 1988. Had the original designation taken place today, many of the buildings we now propose adding would undoubtedly have been included.

When Samuel B. Ruggles created his park in 1831 he laid out Irving Place to be its chief avenue of approach. Many of the original buildings on the street are now, sadly, gone, but many which survive are unprotected, in particular the houses on the west side between 18th and 19th streets. The northernmost and most vulnerable of these has the added distinction of being one of the most successful early-20th-century combinations of commercial and residential use in New York.

Landmark designation of such buildings, however, is only one of the goals of the present survey. As important a purpose is to identify places of architectural, historical, and cultural importance that have lost the attention of the immediate community. Of great importance, for instance, are the large buildings erected between 1892 and 1931 on 22nd Street for major New York charitable institutions. At the northeast corner of Park Avenue South, R. H. Robertson's United Charities Building, recently declared a National Historic Site, is, with its multitude of detail, a superb essay in the rich relationship a large building can have with the street. At the other end of the block, the former Russell Sage Foundation's palazzo by Grosvenor Atterbury is one of the best existing adaptations of Florentine magnificence to New York — a building that knows how to be both huge and intimate in a city street as tight as many in Florence. Its splendid first-floor window grilles sport golden Barberini bees (albeit Roman, not Florentine), and over the former main entrance their hive contains the number 130 of the address surrounded by 53 superb wrought-iron roses.

On 22nd Street between Lexington and Third avenues are a number of other buildings deserving preservation, among them the former Family Courthouse with its aluminum reliefs, the Neo-Flemish carriage house at No. 150, and Gustavus Adolphus Church, designed by the architect of the first Metropolitan Opera House, J. C. Cady.

On Third Avenue at the east side of the district are rows of two- and three-story 19th-century buildings that have long been overlooked. During their 60-odd years under the "el," they were rarely noticed. Now they are exposed to the light again, and their scale and consistency in a stretch of avenue houses are increasingly rare in Manhattan. They include, in fact, many of the earliest buildings in the area — houses with commercial ground floors, some commissioned by Samuel Ruggles himself and erected by his builder, George Furst. When they were built, Third Avenue was a trotting course for fashionable people who lived downtown and took their carriages for drives out of the city. The avenue was later equipped with gaslights on this stretch north of 14th Street, and these little houses with their shops and stables were part of a scene very different from today's. They have survived, however, many of them occupied by the same sort of small shops as a century ago — a continuity quite rare in New York. They deserve to be protected as part of the proposed Gramercy Park Historic District Extension.

A word about the north side of the park itself. It has often been dismissed as unworthy of designation. But this north *wall* of the park has many elements whose loss must be avoided: No. 44, for example, with its leaded-glass and Tudor detail; or No. 60, by the important New York architect Emery Roth — its original windows recently lost, but the wonderful Spanish roof scene still intact: terraces, red tiles, and huge Imperial two-headed eagle guarding the elaborate water tower. This is as essential a part of the Gramercy roofscape as any of its celebrated neighbors.

To the south of the park, in particular on splendid East 17th Street and on Irving Place, are buildings, isolated or in groups, which deserve to be cherished. Whether as a part of the proposed extension, designated individually, or as a small historic district, they must be preserved. For it is hard to imagine the Gramercy Park area without the charming house at 49 Irving Place, long thought erroneously to have been the home of Washington Irving, but later and indisputably that of America's first great interior decorator, Elsie de Wolfe; Scheffel Hall (recently Tuesday's), the wonderful old Rathskeller on Third Avenue, immortalized by O. Henry as "Old Munich"; or 136 East 16th Street with its spectacular Herter ironwork. All are utterly unprotected. They and the other places described in these pages merit the attention and pride of the whole Gramercy community. The politics of official designation are complex today, but that only makes our local care of this treasured New York neighborhood all the more necessary.

Finally, a word about commemorative plaques. Some have already been installed, both in the present historic district and in the proposed additions, but places where many interesting people have lived and worked still go unmarked. On page 92 herein is a list of names and addresses that should be considered for commemorative markers. This would allow our neighborhood to speak its history more effectively.

INTRODUCTION   **ANDREW SCOTT DOLKART**

IN 1966, the New York City Landmarks Preservation Commission designated the relatively small Gramercy Park Historic District, consisting of Gramercy Park itself, the Calvary Church complex on Park Avenue, and 71 buildings on the east, west, and south sides of the park and along several streets to the south; in 1988, the district was expanded with the addition of 36 Gramercy Park East. These buildings are only a portion of what gives the Gramercy Park community its character — there are many other buildings in the neighborhood of great architectural and historical interest. Therefore, Gramercy Neighborhood Associates, Inc., has proposed a significant expansion of the district boundaries, the designation of a 17th Street/Irving Place Historic District, and the designation of a series of individual buildings and of one building interior in the neighborhood (parts of Washington Irving High School).

The buildings proposed for additional landmark designation illustrate important aspects of the development of the Gramercy Park area, including the area's initial development as a prosperous rowhouse neighborhood, its transformation with the appearance of apartment buildings, and the singular development, within the area, of a substantial concentration of buildings that served charitable purposes.

During the initial period of neighborhood development, primarily in the 1840s and 1850s, the streets of Gramercy Park became solidly lined with brick and brownstone rowhouses and mansions, as well as institutional buildings such as churches, that were commonly found in residential areas. As would be expected, the lots facing the private Gramercy Park itself were among the most prestigious places of residence in pre-Civil War New York. Examples of the fine houses erected during this period can still be seen on Gramercy Park West and South, within the designated district.

Rowhouses also lined most of the side streets between 14th and 23rd streets, and a significant number of these still survive on the blocks to the south of the park. Some of these rowhouses are within the designated district, notably those on East 18th and East 19th streets between Irving Place and Third Avenue. Additional rowhouses on East 19th Street are within the proposed Gramercy Park Historic District Extension; others, on East 17th Street, are within the proposed 17th Street/Irving Place Historic District; and a few on East 15th and East 16th streets are being proposed for individual designation. To the north of the park, on East 22nd Street, was a mix of rowhouses and carriage houses, while Lexington Avenue between the park and East 23rd Street contained two mansions. Very little that dates from this early period of development remains to the north or east of the park, with the exception of a series of simple mid-19th-century Greek Revival and early Italianate mixed-use residential/commercial buildings on Third Avenue, all within the proposed Gramercy Park Historic District Extension.

A new period of development in the Gramercy Park area was ushered in in 1869 with the construction of the Stuyvesant Apartments on East 18th Street (demolished). Designed by Richard Morris Hunt, this is generally credited with being the earliest apartment building erected to attract a middle-class clientele.[*] In the 1870s and 1880s, the Stuyvesant was joined by a series of other early apartment houses, notably 129 East 17th Street (1878), thought to be the oldest intact apartment house in the city. Several important multiple dwellings were erected during the 1880s, including the Gramercy at 34 Gramercy Park East (George da Cunha, 1883; within the designated district), one of the earliest cooperatives in New York, and 155 East 22nd Street, designed in 1889 by DeLemos & Cordes, the earliest extant multiple dwelling erected in the section of the neighborhood north of the park.

In the decades that followed, apartment-house construction flourished on East 22nd Street and on Gramercy Park North and, to a lesser extent, on the streets south of the park. Early in the 20th century, two interesting apartment houses joined DeLemos & Cordes' building on 22nd Street between Third and Lexington avenues: Sass & Smallheiser's Beaux-Arts building at 144 East 22nd Street (1901) and Bernstein & Bernstein's unusual building at 152-156 East 22nd Street (1907) with its five stepped gables and extensive terra-cotta detail. In 1912, a multiple dwelling planned specifically for bachelors appeared at 52 Irving Place. This handsome Colonial Revival style structure with suites of rooms that lacked kitchen facilities was one of a small group of New York apartment houses planned for single men in the early years of the 20th century.

During the 1920s, the character of Gramercy Park North was completely transformed as the old rowhouses were replaced by tall luxury apartment houses and a hotel. The first apartment house along the park's northern face was 1 Lexington Avenue, begun in 1910. Between 1926 and 1929, three additional large-scale apartment houses were begun on Gramercy Park North, and in 1924 work began on the Gramercy Park Hotel at the northwest corner of Gramercy Park North and Lexington Avenue; the hotel was extended in 1929-30, completing the transformation of this park frontage. Contemporary with the Gramercy Park North buildings is the flamboyant apartment house at 81 Irving Place, northwest corner East 19th Street, designed by George Pelham and ornamented with fantastical terra-cotta detail.

---

[*] Elizabeth Collins Cromley, *Alone Together: A History of New York's Early Apartments* (Ithaca: Cornell University Press, 1990), pp. 73-83.

In the second and third decades of the 20th century, during the time when many of the large apartment houses were being developed on Gramercy Park, a change occurred in the design and use of many of the surviving side-street rowhouses. By the early 20th century, few of these houses were being maintained as single-family dwellings. The affluent families who had inhabited them had moved elsewhere, and the Gramercy Park neighborhood lost some of its social standing. Most of the rowhouses were converted into boarding houses or into apartments. Many of the houses had their facades redesigned, as occurred on East 19th Street within the historic district, or underwent less radical changes, such as the removal of a stoop (this facilitated the rearrangement of the interiors for apartment use). Although the facades of many of the surviving rowhouses located to the south of the park remain intact, others exhibit these early-20th-century alterations.

The changing character of the neighborhood caused by the movement of prosperous residents to other areas had a second result, the redevelopment of certain sites into loft and factory buildings. Commercial redevelopment moved eastward, into the Gramercy Park neighborhood, from the Ladies' Mile along Broadway. By the early 20th century, loft buildings were being erected on Fourth Avenue (now Park Avenue South) and on many of the adjacent side streets, appearing as far east as Irving Place.

The most interesting development to the north of Gramercy Park was the transformation of the area just south of 23rd Street into a center for charitable institutions. In the late 19th century, New York's charitable organizations grew in number and size, in response to the growing interest that middle- and upper-class reformers had in attempting to change conditions in the city's growing poor and immigrant communities. The reformers established or invigorated organizations that furthered new developments in housing, health, education, social work, and other fields and offered charity to certain poor people in need. Their work represents the explosion of organized efforts by affluent citizens to effect change in the city. Not all of the efforts of these reformers led to positive changes, but they were able to accomplish many important reforms which set the stage for much of 20th-century American social policy.

The growth of the charitable organizations and the expansion of their missions led to a corresponding growth in the number and scale of buildings erected to serve the needs of both the organizations and the city's needy population. In the last years of the 19th century and first decades of the 20th century, progressive reformers successfully petitioned for an increase in the number of schools, parks, public baths, courts, and other civic structures, and they built settlement houses for the poor and office buildings to meet their own needs. There are four buildings in the proposed historic-district extension that were built to house the headquarters of important institutions — the United Charities Building, the Association for the Prevention of Cruelty to Children Building, the Church Missions House (a designated individual landmark), all built in 1892-93, and the Russell Sage Foundation Building, built initially in 1912-15 and extended in 1929-31. The Gramercy Park area may have attracted these charitable institutions because it remained a respectable neighborhood, it was centrally located and convenient to mass-transit lines, and land was less expensive here than in newly fashionable areas to the north.

In addition to the headquarters buildings for philanthropic organizations, four buildings were erected as centers of progressive social programs — the Manhattan Trade School for Girls (1915-19), the Children's Court (1912-1916), and the Domestic Relations Court's Family Court Building (1937-39) are all within the boundaries of the proposed historic district extension, while Washington Irving High School is in the proposed 17th Street/Irving Place Historic District. Each of the buildings erected for charitable or civic purposes is of historical and/or architectural interest in its own right; together they create an extremely important complex of major social-service buildings.

The designation of the proposed historic district extension, and of the additional district and series of individual buildings, as proposed by Gramercy Neighborhood Associates, Inc., will preserve the comprehensive history of the architectural and social development of Gramercy Park.

What follows is a discussion of each of the buildings that is being proposed for landmark designation, either as part of a historic district or as an individual landmark. Part I is a presentation of each of the buildings in the proposed Gramercy Park Historic District Extension. The buildings on Gramercy Park are listed first, followed by buildings to the north of the park (on Lexington Avenue, Park Avenue South, and East 22nd Street), to the east of the park (on Third Avenue), and to the south of the park (on East 19th Street and Irving Place). Part II is a presentation of the proposed 17th Street/Irving Place Historic District. The discussion of buildings in this small district is presented in a generally chronological manner beginning with the rowhouses of the 1840s and ending with the International style office building erected by the Guardian Life Insurance Company. Finally, Part III presents the proposed individual landmarks, arranged geographically from north to south. An Index and Table of Contents are provided to assist in the convenient location of information on each structure.

GNA Archives

UNITED CHARITIES BUILDING
Park Avenue South at 22nd Street, looking northeast, as it appeared when first built in 1892. The A.S.P.C.A.
headquarters, demolished that year, appears at right
(See page 31)

PART ONE
PROPOSED GRAMERCY PARK
HISTORIC DISTRICT EXTENSION

GRAMERCY PARK EAST

GRAMERCY PARK NORTH

LEXINGTON AVENUE

PARK AVENUE SOUTH

EAST 22ND STREET

THIRD AVENUE

EAST 19TH STREET

IRVING PLACE

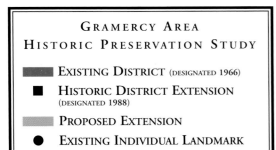

GRAMERCY AREA
HISTORIC PRESERVATION STUDY

■ EXISTING DISTRICT (DESIGNATED 1966)

■ HISTORIC DISTRICT EXTENSION
(DESIGNATED 1988)

■ PROPOSED EXTENSION

● EXISTING INDIVIDUAL LANDMARK

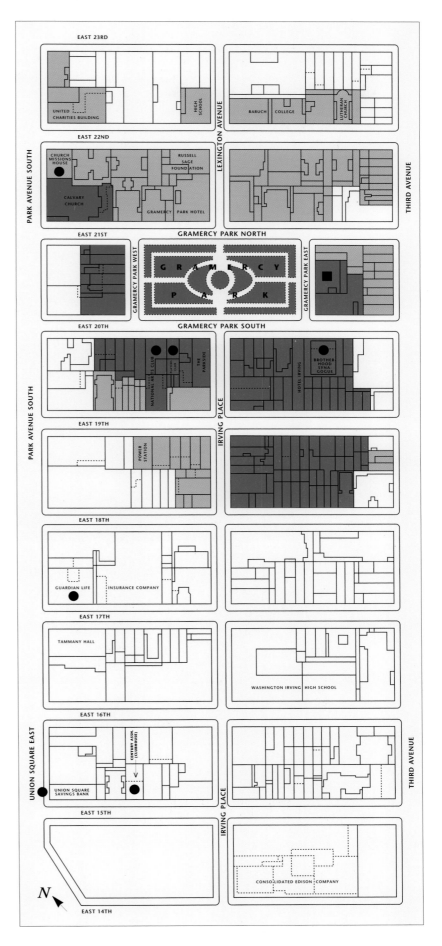

UNITED CHARITIES BUILDING
No. 105 East 22nd Street
Entrance detail

GRAMERCY PARK EAST

GRAMERCY PARK EAST BETWEEN GRAMERCY PARK SOUTH
AND GRAMERCY PARK NORTH

Truman Moore

Truman Moore

37 GRAMERCY PARK EAST
Architect: unknown
Date: 1853-54; altered, 1968

38 GRAMERCY PARK EAST
Architect: unknown
Date: 1853-54; redesigned, c.1920

THE EAST SIDE of Gramercy Park was developed in the mid-1850s. Soon after its completion, the Anglo-Italianate rowhouse erected at No. 37 became part of Sanderson's Family Hotel, which stretched along most of Gramercy Park East. By 1866, the hotel was known as Gramercy Park House. An 1866 guidebook describes the establishment, somewhat grandiosely, as "one of the largest hotels in the city, built of substantial brown stone, and in one of the most aristocratic localities of Gotham. In its internal arrangements it is unsurpassed and contains spacious accommodations for six to eight hundred guests."[1] The Anglo-Italianate features evident on the first floor of this building include rusticated stonework and a pair of arched openings reconstructed when the upper floors were modernized in 1968.

BUILT IN 1853-54 as one of several buildings along Gramercy Park East that, soon after their completion, became Sanderson's Family Hotel, this structure has undergone a succession of alterations in design and use. According to New York City Buildings Department records, the building was a private residence in 1885, but by 1891 had again been converted into a hotel; by 1913 this was a boarding house, and by 1926 it contained 35 non-housekeeping apartments (e.g., apartments without kitchens). The present Neo-Tudor facade, with its pseudo-half-timbered upper floors and oriel, its crenelated roofline, and metal casement windows, probably dates from about 1920 when a number of old rowhouses in New York were being redesigned with mock-medieval facades.

1. *New York As It Is; or Stranger's Guide-Book to the Cities of New York, Brooklyn and Adjacent Places* (New York: J. Miller, 1866), p. 69.

GRAMERCY PARK NORTH

60 GRAMERCY PARK NORTH

2 LEXINGTON AVENUE
Gramercy Park Hotel

NORTH WALL OF BUILDINGS AT GRAMERCY PARK
Between Park Avenue South and Third Avenue

In the background, beyond the trees, is the north side of Gramercy Park as seen from Irving Place
at Gramercy Park South. At extreme left the tower of Metropolitan Life Insurance Co. (Madison Avenue at 24th
Street); then left to right, No. 60 Gramercy Park North, No. 2 Lexington Avenue (Gramercy Park Hotel), No. 1
Lexington Avenue, Nos. 48, 45, 44, and 40 Gramercy Park North.

45 GRAMERCY PARK NORTH

1 LEXINGTON AVENUE

44 GRAMERCY PARK NORTH

Truman Moore

48 GRAMERCY PARK NORTH

40 GRAMERCY PARK NORTH

GRAMERCY PARK NORTH

Truman Moore

40 GRAMERCY PARK NORTH
Architect: unknown
Date: 1852-53

No. 40 GRAMERCY PARK NORTH is a survivor from the initial period of development around the park. The Anglo-Italianate brownstone-fronted dwelling was built as part of a row. As was characteristic of Anglo-Italianate houses, this residence has a low stoop leading to an arched entrance. A projecting balcony separates the entrance level from the upper floors, which are articulated by segmental-arched wooden casement windows that become shorter on each successive floor. The building is crowned by its original wooden cornice with ornate fascia board.

44 GRAMERCY PARK NORTH
Architect: Schwartz & Gross
Date: 1929-30

The architects, Schwartz & Gross, were among the most prolific apartment-house designers of the early decades of the 20th century. During the 1910s and most of the 1920s, Schwartz & Gross designed buildings with Renaissance-inspired detail, but in the late 1920s, the firm began to use medieval features, as is evident on this building and on such contemporary designs as 14 East 75th Street (1928-29) and 1185 Park Avenue (1928).

NO. 44 GRAMERCY PARK NORTH
Detail of windows

I N ITS MASSING, this large apartment house appears as two separate structures, reflecting the different height restrictions required by New York's zoning code for buildings erected on a side street and opposite a park. The section of 44 Gramercy Park North situated opposite the open space of the park rises to a height of 15 stories, but the section facing onto East 21st Street was allowed to rise only to a height of 90 feet, or nine stories. The building facade is unified in its use of materials and ornamental details. The entire facade is faced in brick and has an overlay of Neo-Gothic detail that includes a limestone pointed-arch entry and large leaded-glass window on the ground floor, and, on the upper floors, white terra-cotta panels with buttresses and blind pointed arches, terra-cotta balconies pierced by quatrefoils, drip lintels, modest gables, and crenelated parapets. In addition, the three upper floors of both sections of the building are enlivened with brick diaperwork, and all of the windows retain their original multi-paned metal casements.

NO. 44 GRAMERCY PARK NORTH
Detail of balcony and windows

No. 45 Gramercy Park North

45 GRAMERCY PARK NORTH
Architect: G.A. & H. Boehm
Date: 1926-27

NO. 45 GRAMERCY PARK NORTH
Detail of service entrance

GEORGE A. AND HENRY BOEHM, architects best known for their design of the *Jewish Daily Forward* building on East Broadway, designed this simple Neo-Renaissance 16-story apartment building to house 32 families, two on each floor. The building has a stone base highlighted by an unusual entrance pediment, ornamented with babies carved in relief. The upper floors are faced with brick and massed with a series of setbacks.

NO. 45 GRAMERCY PARK NORTH
Detail of window grille

NO. 45 GRAMERCY PARK NORTH
Detail of main entrance

48 GRAMERCY PARK NORTH (*Not shown*)
Architect: original building, unknown; alterations, Lucien
      David and Jack Pickens Coble
Date: original building, 1858; altered, 1958 and 1968

IN 1958, the original 1858 rowhouse received a new brick facade. Ten years later the park frontage was embellished with a three-story veranda, and new French doors and casement windows were installed. For many years this was the home of Peter Cooper's grandson, Edward Hewitt (c.1867-1957). Hewitt, a Trustee of Gramercy Park, was a prominent inventor, responsible, for example, for a particularly sticky glue he invented while working in Peter Cooper's glue factory and for the original motor used in Mack trucks.

NO. 60 GRAMERCY PARK NORTH
Seen from Gramercy Park West

60 GRAMERCY PARK NORTH/120 EAST 22ND STREET
Architect: Emery Roth
Date: 1928

THE TALENTED apartment-house architect Emery Roth was responsible for the design of this large building with wings facing both Gramercy Park and East 22nd Street. The beige brick building, with limestone-fronted base, Renaissance-inspired terra-cotta detail, and rooftop water-tower pavilion, resembles other important Roth works of the late 1920s. The building is unusual for its use of Spanish as well as Italian architectural motifs. Of special interest are the Spanish tiles that appear on the building's cornice and on the roof of the water-tower pavilion. Ornament is used on the facades to accent the base, setbacks, and roofline. This use of ornate decoration on only a few sections of the building is typical of Roth's finest designs. Here, twisted and bulbous columns, strapwork, shells, and eagles decorate the strategic portions of the street facades. In his monograph on Roth, Steven Ruttenbaum notes that "it was Roth's intention that his sixteen-story building enhance the refined character of the neighborhood."[2]

2. Steven Ruttenbaum, *Mansions in the Clouds: The Skyscraper Palazzi of Emery Roth* (New York: Balsam Press, 1986), p. 87.

22

No. 60 Gramercy Park North
Water-tower pavilion

No. 60 Gramercy Park North
Water-tower pavilion and penthouses, looking northeast

No. 60 Gramercy Park North
Detail of main entrance

No. 60 Gramercy Park North
Detail of windows

23

LEXINGTON AVENUE

LEXINGTON AVENUE, EAST SIDE, BETWEEN GRAMERCY PARK
NORTH AND EAST 22ND STREET

Truman Moore

NO. 1 LEXINGTON AVENUE, in 1993
Showing streetlamp since replaced by bishop's-crook lamp

1 LEXINGTON AVENUE
Architect: Herbert Lucas
Date: 1910-11

THE 12-STORY apartment house at the corner of Gramercy Park North and Lexington Avenue is the earliest of the apartment houses that line the north side of the park. The building was one of three luxury cooperatives erected on the park between 1908 and 1910. Architect Herbert Lucas was responsible for two of these—24 Gramercy Park South and 1 Lexington Avenue.[3] These cooperatives were planned with sizable apartments to attract an affluent and artistic group of people who were interested in living in well-designed apartment houses in a cultured and respectable neighborhood, albeit one located at some distance from the city's most elite residences on the Upper East Side. The development of these cooperative buildings coincided with the artistic "modernization" of rowhouses on East 19th Street, just south of the park.

No. 1 Lexington Avenue was one of a series of cooperatives erected early in the 20th century that were known as "club" buildings. Club or cooperative buildings were seen as being advantageous because they provided residents with the amenities of a private home without the problems attendant on owning an individual residence. The *Real Estate Record and Builders Guide* suggested that 1 Lexington Avenue would, "in its private ownership and in its exclusive character, as well as in the possession of certain lineaments and conveniences, have an attractiveness analogous to that of a private home."[4]

No. 1 Lexington Avenue is a well-proportioned brick building with a two-story limestone base. It has an especially imposing entrance with a projecting limestone portico supported by Tuscan columns. This portico is an enlarged version of that designed by Stanford White in 1899-1901 for his alterations to 49-50 Gramercy Park North (123 East 21st Street) undertaken for Henry W. Poor; this was the house demolished to make way for the construction of 1 Lexington Avenue.[5] Above the portico are round-arched windows embellished with finely carved garlands of fruit. The brick on the upper floors is laid in Flemish bond with burned headers creating a lively pattern of light and dark. The building is surrounded by an especially handsome fence consisting of tall narrow rounded pickets. The fence, designed by Stanford White, was salvaged during the demolition of the Poor mansion.

3. Lucas trained in the office of McKim, Mead & White as well as in Paris and became an associate partner in the McKim, Mead & White firm. He designed several other apartment houses in New York as well as a variety of other buildings (see New York City Landmarks Preservation Commission, *Upper East Side Historic District Designation Report*, Vol. II [1981], p. 1287). The third cooperative from this period is 36 Gramercy Park East (1908-10) designed by James Riely Gordon; this structure, now a rental building, was added to the Gramercy Park Historic District in 1988.

4. "Number One Lexington Avenue," *Real Estate Record and Builders Guide* 85 (May 21, 1910), p. 1085.

5. Henry Poor commissioned Stanford White to alter the house that had been built for Cyrus Field and in which Field had planned the Atlantic Cable. This is commemorated on a plaque that is on the building.

Photographer Unknown

NO. 1 LEXINGTON AVENUE, C. 1910
Showing, to the left, Peter Cooper's house at No. 9

PARK GRAMERCY (*Not shown*)
7 Lexington Avenue
Architect: Boak & Raad
Date: 1949-51

THE THIRTEEN-STORY building at the southeast corner of Lexington Avenue and East 22nd Street is a very late example of a building with Art Deco forms. It is faced with the pale yellow brick often used on Art Deco apartment houses and contains metal sash windows and a multi-tiered aluminum awning with the name of the building spelled out on top. The building was planned to contain 94 small apartments and four doctors' offices. This apartment house replaces the home of Peter Cooper, as noted on the plaque attached to the building.

GRAMERCY PARK HOTEL, in 1993
Seen through the north gates of the park

GRAMERCY PARK HOTEL
2 Lexington Avenue
Architect: Robert T. Lyons; extension on Gramercy Park
        North, Thompson & Churchill
Date: 1924-25; extension, 1929-30

THE LARGE GRAMERCY PARK HOTEL was erected in two building campaigns. The earlier section is that located at the corner of Gramercy Park North and Lexington Avenue, replacing the former Stanford White house.[6] Four years after the initial 16-story hotel was completed, it was extended westward along the park frontage. Both sections of the Gramercy Park Hotel are extremely simple Renaissance Revival style brick structures with a two-story stone base topped by balustrade railings. The Gramercy Park has long been a popular residential hotel; among those who lived at the hotel were Joseph P. Kennedy and his family (including the 11-year-old John F. Kennedy), who occupied the second floor for several months just after the hotel opened; S.J. Perelman, who lived and died in Room 1621; and Edmund Wilson and Mary McCarthy, who resided in the hotel during the 1940s. Humphrey Bogart was married here in 1926.

6. Four fireplaces salvaged from White's house were installed in the new hotel. These fireplaces were not designed by White, but apparently date from the 1847 house that White remodeled.

Photographer Unknown

NO. 2 LEXINGTON AVENUE
Gramercy Park Hotel
In 1925 when just built

PARK AVENUE SOUTH

PARK AVENUE SOUTH, EAST SIDE, BETWEEN EAST 21ST AND
EAST 23ND STREETS

NEW YORK SOCIETY
FOR THE PREVENTION OF CRUELTY
TO CHILDREN

UNITED CHARITIES BUILDING

CHURCH MISSIONS HOUSE

NEW YORK SOCIETY FOR THE PREVENTION OF CRUELTY TO CHILDREN
295 Park Avenue South

CHURCH MISSIONS HOUSE
        (now Federation of Protestant Welfare Agencies)
281 Park Avenue South
Architect: Robert Gibson
Date: 1892-94

THIS MAGNIFICENT steel-framed building, with its light-hued stone street facade, is a designated individual landmark. The building was designed to house the offices of the Episcopal Church's mission activities. The architect, Robert Gibson, was a talented designer with the ability to create successful buildings in many different styles: the Church Missions House is modeled on the Renaissance guild halls of Flemish cities; his St. Michael's Episcopal Church on Amsterdam Avenue and West 99th Street is a dramatic Romanesque Revival structure; the Morton Plant House (now Cartier's) on Fifth Avenue and East 52nd Street is an Italian Renaissance-inspired dwelling; while Gibson's most famous building, West End Collegiate Church on West End Avenue and West 77th Street, is an adaptation of the Dutch Renaissance Butcher's Market in the city of Haarlem.

NEW YORK SOCIETY FOR THE PREVENTION
OF CRUELTY TO CHILDREN
295 Park Avenue South
Architect: Renwick, Aspinwall & Renwick
Date: 1892

THE NEW YORK SOCIETY for the Prevention of Cruelty to Children was organized in 1875 in response to a law passed in that year by the New York State Legislature authorizing the establishment of branches of this child-welfare organization in each county of the state. The organization was established to investigate cases of cruelty to children under the age of 16, to care for abused children, and to assist in the enforcement of laws established to protect children.

The Society's building on the southeast corner of Park Avenue South and East 23rd Street was begun in 1892, the same year that work began on the adjoining United Charities Building *(see page 30)*. It is clear from the restrained exterior design that the Society for the Prevention of Cruelty to Children did not wish to expend a great deal of unnecessary money on the embellishment of their new headquarters. The building has an unadorned stone base, a simple yellow brick upper facade, and modest terra-cotta detail. The major ornamental features are located on the seventh floor, where terra-cotta panels with figures of children represent the original use of the building. These panels are modeled after those designed by Andrea Della Robbia at the Ospedale degli Innocenti in Florence. This terra-cotta work was created by the Perth Amboy Terra Cotta Company. The main entrance, located in the center of the Park Avenue South elevation, was originally set within a projecting two-story portico with freestanding columns, but this entrance has been cut back to the building line. The building has been converted into apartments.

NO. 295 PARK AVENUE SOUTH
Detail above main entrance

NO. 295 PARK AVENUE SOUTH
Showing terra-cotta panels of seventh floor

East 22nd Street

East 22nd Street, North Side, between
Park Avenue South and Lexington Avenue

Truman Moore

United Charities Building
105 East 22nd Street
Architect: R.H. Robertson with Rowe & Baker; additions,
    James Baker
Date: 1892; additions, 1897, 1915

Church Missions House
(Now Federation of Protestant
Welfare Agencies)

THE CONSTRUCTION OF the United Charities Building in 1892 was an important milestone in the history of philanthropy in New York. The building was erected for use as the headquarters of four prominent charitable institutions, the Charity Organization Society, the Association for Improving the Condition of the Poor, the Children's Aid Society, and the New York Mission and Tract Society. It was planned as a response to the fact that office rental costs were becoming an ever-increasing burden for charitable organizations. The idea of opening a building to house several charitable organizations had first been broached in 1885, but nothing was done about this proposal until 1890, when a subscription was started by the Charity Organization Society to raise funds for the erection of such a structure. A year later, John S. Kennedy, a wealthy banker involved with several charitable groups, offered to pay the entire cost of the site and building.

Kennedy chose R.H. Robertson as architect for the project. Robertson was an appropriate choice, having had extensive experience with the design of buildings for charitable and religious institutions, including the YWCA at 7 East 15th Street and the related Margaret Louisa Home at 14-16

East 16th Street (both in the Ladies' Mile Historic District) and the Academy of Medicine on West 43rd Street (demolished). Robertson was assisted by the firm of Rowe & Baker; James Baker was Kennedy's nephew.[7] It is generally believed that Robertson was fully responsible for the exterior of the United Charities Building, which was designed in the Renaissance Revival mode that he had begun to use early in the 1890s. Baker may have been responsible for some of the interiors. The most important interior space, the ground-floor Assembly Hall, entered directly from an entrance at the east end of the 22nd Street elevation, is undoubtedly Robertson's work. Although somewhat deteriorated, this room is an extraordinary survivor from the late 19th century. It contains a cast-iron coved ceiling, supporting piers, plaster foliate decoration, plaster roundels with children's heads, and a speaker's platform.

The original United Charities Building was a seven-story structure with a two-story limestone base, four-story brick central section divided into two two-story units, and a crowning mansard roof over the entire East 22nd Street elevation and half of the Park Avenue South frontage. The main entrance was through a wide round arch on East 22nd

Street, but there were subsidiary entrances on Park Avenue South (known as Fourth Avenue at the time the building was constructed). On Park Avenue South, the building was divided internally into two sections, each with a separate entrance (after Kennedy's death in 1909 the section to the north was named the Kennedy Building). In 1897, James Baker was commissioned to remove the mansard and add three additional stories to the entire structure. Baker received additional work in 1915, when he designed the four-story addition at 111 East 22nd Street that was planned to provide space for the New York School of Philanthropy.

The main section of the United Charities Building still houses philanthropic institutions, notably the Community Service Society, formed in 1939 by the merger of the Charity Organization Society and the Association for Improving the Condition of the Poor. The Kennedy Building and the 22nd Street extension have been sold. The Kennedy Building is now apartments. In 1946, the extension became the headquarters of the Dockbuilder's Union. In the 1980s, the union sold the building and it underwent a conversion for commercial use (it became a restaurant and modeling agency). In 1991, the entire United Charities complex was designated a National Historic Landmark.

7. John S. Kennedy was able to assist his nephew in receiving several important design commissions other than the United Charities Building. These include the Chamber of Commerce on Liberty Street (Kennedy was an active member) and the Presbyterian Building on Fifth Avenue and West 20th Street (Kennedy was a Presbyterian) in the Ladies' Mile Historic District.

No. 105 East 22nd Street
Entrance on 22nd Street

No. 105 East 22nd Street
Window bay detail

United Charities Building
Park Avenue South at 22nd Street, as it appeared when first built in 1892. The A.S.P.C.A. headquarters, demolished that year, appears to the right

MANHATTAN TRADE SCHOOL FOR GIRLS
(now The New Manhattan High School Collaborative)
No. 127 East 22nd Street
Looking northwest

32

MANHATTAN TRADE SCHOOL FOR GIRLS
(now The New Manhattan High School Collaborative)
127 East 22nd Street
Architect: C.B.J. Snyder
Date: 1915-19

THE MANHATTAN TRADE SCHOOL for Girls was established as a private philanthropy in 1902 with the aim of teaching skills to working girls so that these girls could gain employment in jobs where they would be paid a decent wage; the school also ensured that skilled labor would be available to New York's businesses. According to the school's *First Annual Report*, this was "an experiment without precedent."[8] The school was supported by a combination of wealthy New York men and women with an interest in charitable pursuits and a group of professionals involved with a variety of reform endeavors. The school was originally located on West 14th Street, moving to East 23rd Street in about 1907. In response to the increasing demand for vocational education, the New York City school system absorbed the Manhattan Trade School and it became one of four vocational schools in the city and the only one that admitted female students.[9]

The curriculum established in 1902 remained fairly constant through the early years of city operation. Classes were offered in a variety of trades, almost all connected to the fact that New York was the center of America's garment-making industry. Instruction was offered in three basic areas: needle or tool trades where students were taught millinery, fine garment making, and dressmaking; electric power machine operating trades including training in the manufacture of clothing and straw goods (notably hats) as well as in embroidery; and the pasting trades, including training young women in labeling and sample mounting and in the manufacturing of pocketbooks, card-cases, and novelty boxes. Special courses were also offered in embroidery design and embroidery pattern perforation.

According to those who ran the school, these trades were chosen because

> [they] employ large numbers of women. They require expert workers; training for them is difficult to obtain. They are well paid; favorable conditions prevail in the workrooms and there is chance for promotion to better pay.[10]

This view of conditions and opportunities in the factories where graduates might have been employed appears to be somewhat rosier than reality, but this school was an important commitment, first by private individuals and later by the city, to train young women for trades in which they might be able to make an adequate income.

At the time that the Manhattan Trade School for Girls became part of the public-school system, students attended classes for seven hours a day. Five hours each day were spent in trade practice; 1½ hours were spent studying nonvocational subjects that could be applied to trade work, such as English, arithmetic, and textile design; and 30 minutes a day were spent in hygiene and gymnastics class.[11]

The demand for admittance to this free city school was so great that a larger building was needed. Designs for the new building were begun in 1914, and plans were approved by the New York City Art Commission in 1915.[12] In that year, the principal of the school recommended "that strenuous effort be made to have the new building ready for occupancy at the earliest possible moment. Under the present conditions the progress of the trade school is being steadily impaired, since it is impossible, with continuous overcrowding, not only to do the present work efficiently, but also to undertake new lines of activity until better accommodations are provided."[13]

The school was designed by C.B.J. Snyder, the city's Superintendent of School Buildings and the architect responsible for the design of a large number of New York's most important school buildings. The Manhattan Trade School's home is among the most unusual early-20th-century school buildings in the city. For this building, Snyder was faced with demands to design a public-school building, but one with space needs that were considerably different from those of most schools. Snyder designed a building in the Collegiate Gothic mode, "similar to that of the other school buildings erected by the city during recent years."[14] Snyder excelled in the use of this style, designing New York's finest Collegiate Gothic schools, including Morris, Erasmus Hall, Flushing, and Curtis high schools. At the Manhattan Trade School, the collegiate imagery was applied to a loftlike structure. In addition, figures at the cornice level hold books and tools. This combination of a loftlike structure with collegiate imagery was appropriate for a school where students were trained in trades that were largely carried out in industrial lofts.

With the exception of the limestone ground floor, the building is entirely clad in white terra cotta. At the time of its completion, this was the tallest school building in the city. It had stores on the ground floor (initial plans called for a sales room and restaurant). On the second floor was a large lecture hall, on the top floor a gymnasium, and on the intermediate floors a series of workrooms. The terra-cotta facades have recently been restored and, except for the loss of the rooftop parapet and original window sash, the building remains as built. It still functions as a city high school, although no longer a vocational school for girls.

8. Manhattan Trade School for Girls, *First Annual Report* (1904), p. 6.

9. The other vocational schools were the Vocational School for Boys, Murray Hill Vocational School for Boys, and Brooklyn Vocational School for Boys.

10. *First Annual Report,* p. 9.

11. *Preparing Girls for Trades: Report of Manhattan Trade School for Girls* (1914-15), p. 15.

12. "Manhattan Trade School for Girls," Art Commission File #860.

13. Ibid., p. 48.

14. "Manhattan Trade School for Girls," *Real Estate Record and Builders Guide* 99 (May 12, 1917), p. 669.

120

102

GRAMERCY ARMS
102 East 22nd Street
Architect: Sugarman & Berger
Date: 1928

G RAMERCY ARMS is a 10-story Art Deco building designed by an architectural firm that specialized in middle-class apartment houses. Much of Sugarman & Berger's work, including several examples within the Upper West Side/Central Park West Historic District, was designed in the Neo-Renaissance style, but beginning in the late 1920s, the firm's designs began to show the influence of the newly popular Art Deco; this includes the former Hotel New Yorker on Eighth Avenue and West 34th Street and the Broadway Fashion Building on Broadway and West 84th Street. Of special note on the 22nd Street building are the polychromatic glazed terra-cotta panels located below the second-, fifth-, seventh-, and ninth-floor levels.

120 EAST 22ND STREET

T HIS STRUCTURE IS the northern section of the apartment house at 60 Gramercy Park North *(see page 22)* designed by Emery Roth in 1928. The Building extends through the block, with its East 22nd Street closely resembling, in materials and detail, the front elevation on Gramercy Park.

RUSSELL SAGE FOUNDATION
(now Sage House)
Nos. 122-130 East 22nd Street (4 Lexington Avenue).
Looking southwest, showing 10th floor added in the early 1920s
and the 16-story extension added in 1929-31

RUSSELL SAGE FOUNDATION
Soon after it was finished in 1915, looking southwest;
Stanford White's former house seen to the left

RUSSELL SAGE FOUNDATION
Entrance at 130 East 22nd Street, showing frieze descriptive
of the work of the Russell Sage Foundation for which
the building was built

Enlarged detail

RUSSELL SAGE FOUNDATION
(now Sage House)
122-130 East 22nd Street (4 Lexington Avenue)
Architect: Grosvenor Atterbury
Date: 1912-15; extension at 122 East 22nd Street, 1929-31

THE RUSSELL SAGE Foundation was founded in 1907 by Margaret O. Sage as a memorial to her husband, the prominent politician and Wall Street financier who had died in 1906.[15] The foundation was established with an initial endowment of $10,000,000 and the goal of promoting the improvement of social and living conditions for the poor. The Russell Sage Foundation was active in the development of social work and urban planning as professions, published many books and articles about social welfare, and sponsored and supported many progressive activities. The foundation is also known for Forest Hills Gardens, a model housing project conceived in 1908. The architect for Forest Hills Gardens, Grosvenor Atterbury, was also commissioned to design the foundation's headquarters.

Following the organization of the foundation, office accommodation was sought in the United Charities Building (see page 30) on East 22nd Street and Park Avenue South, but since this building was fully occupied, space was rented in several buildings in the surrounding area. In 1912, Mrs. Sage and her leading adviser, Robert de Forest, chose to build a headquarters building that would be a physical memorial to Russell Sage. The site at the corner of Lexington Avenue and East 22nd Street was purchased, and Grosvenor Atterbury was commissioned to design the new nine-story building (a 10th-floor penthouse was added in the early 1920s).

Since the new headquarters building was planned as a memorial, more money was spent on the design and construction than would have been appropriate if it had simply been built to house the offices of the charitable group. The street elevations are clad in a particularly beautiful rough-cut red sandstone, known as Kingwood stone, thought to have been used only once before in New York (at the synod house at the Cathedral of St. John the Divine). For the Russell Sage Foundation, Atterbury adapted the form of a Florentine Renaissance palazzo to the needs of a modern office building. The street elevations display the tripartite horizontal massing and rhythmic arrangement of openings that is typical of Florentine palazzi.

A particularly interesting feature of the building is the use of carved panels symbolic of the ideals and goals of the foundation. Located on the second floor, these panels, each in the form of a shield, represent health, work, play, housing, religion, education, civics, and justice. Above the former main entrance, on 22nd Street, is a rectangular panel representing the specialized work of the organization — study, service, and counsel. This use of ornamentation to communicate symbolically the purpose of a building was popular among Beaux-Arts-trained architects such as Atterbury, and is evident on many late-19th- and early-20th-century public and institutional buildings in New York City. These panels are early examples of the architectural sculpture of René Chambellan, a sculptor better known for his later installations at Rockefeller Center and the Chanin Building.

The foundation's new building not only housed the offices of the Russell Sage Foundation, but also contained offices of other social-service organizations, including the American Association of Social Workers and the Family Welfare Association of America. The charitable organizations housed in this building received their space at no charge. The two top floors of the building housed the Social Work Library, one of the finest libraries of its type. In 1929, the foundation decided to expand the building by erecting a wing on East 22nd Street that was to be a profitable venture with space rented to social-service organizations. Atterbury designed a wing that would complement his original structure. The 16-story addition is connected to the original building by a five-story hyphen. The construction of a low building on the midblock site was required by a covenant attached to the deed by the site's prior owner, the Gramercy Park Hotel, who wished to preserve the light entering the hotel rooms that faced north. The New York School of Social Work became the primary tenant of the addition.

In 1949, the Russell Sage Foundation moved from this building and it was sold to the Archdiocese of New York, which used the structure to house the offices of Catholic Charities. In 1975, the building was sold again, and it was subsequently converted into apartments.

---

15. The history of the Russell Sage Foundation and its building is based on Karen Johnson's "Russell Sage Foundation Building," an unpublished paper prepared for Columbia University School of Architecture (1987).

Truman Moore

DOMESTIC RELATIONS COURT, FAMILY COURT BUILDING
    (now Baruch College)
135 East 22nd Street
Architect: Charles B. Meyers
Date: 1937-39

THE DOMESTIC RELATIONS Court Act of the City of New York, passed by the New York State Legislature in 1933, combined the Family Court and Children's Court into the Domestic Relations Court. With the creation of a new court system, the Children's Court located at 137 East 22nd Street *(see page 41)* needed additional room. In 1937, New York City commissioned a new building for court and administrative purposes from architect Charles B. Meyers. Meyers worked extensively for New York City, especially during the 1930s, designing the Criminal Courts Building (with Harvey Wiley Corbett), the Department of Health Building, and several hospitals.

The Domestic Relations Court was established so that the problems of children and of families could be treated in a unified manner.[16] This reflects the continuation of an interest in treating problem children and unstable families in a humane manner that had initially led to the establishment of Children's Court in 1902.

For the new Domestic Relations Court Building, Meyers designed in the austere stripped-down style often referred to as "Modern Classic."[17] The courthouse has a two-story granite base with limestone above. Windows are arranged in vertical bands with aluminum spandrels and are flanked by vertical strips of stone that allude to classical pilasters. In a manner that is characteristic of public buildings erected during the 1930s, the Domestic Relations Court is embellished with a series of reliefs expressing themes exemplifying the use of the structure. These aluminum reliefs, done by sculptor H.P. Camden, are located in the spandrels between the first- and second-floor windows. There are eight figural relief panels, most with family groups involved in activities such as reading, gardening, and praying. Between each of the figural reliefs are abstract foliate motifs that are identical. Over the entrance, Camden designed a panel with the seal of the Domestic Relations Court. This is set in front of an aluminum grille. Although the building has been converted for use by Baruch College, its exterior is virtually unchanged.

16. See Alfred J. Kahn, *A Court for Children: A Study of the New York City Children's Court* (New York: Columbia University Press, 1953).

17. See Robert Stern, Gregory Gilmartin, and Thomas Mellins, *New York 1930: Architecture and Urbanism Between the Two World Wars* (New York: Rizzoli, 1987), pp. 23-26.

Enlarged detail

No. 135 East 22nd Street
Showing one of the aluminum spandrel reliefs
designed by H.P. Camden

CHILDREN'S COURT
(now Baruch College)
No. 137 East 22nd Street

CHILDREN'S COURT
    (now Baruch College)
137 East 22nd Street
Architect: Crow, Lewis & Wickenhoefer
Date: 1912-16

AMONG THE ISSUES that were of concern to the progressive reformers active at the turn of the century was the treatment of juvenile delinquents. Children who were accused of crimes were treated by the court system as adults, with little concern for their age or for their family circumstances. The country's first juvenile-court statute was enacted in Illinois in 1899. The Chicago Bar Association voiced the view that was to take hold in other states, such as New York, that established children's courts:

> The fundamental idea of the Juvenile Court Law is that the State must step in and exercise guardianship over a child found under such adverse social or individual conditions as develop crime....It proposes a plan whereby he may be treated, not as a criminal,...but as a ward of the State, to receive practically the care, custody and discipline that are accorded the neglected and dependent child, and which, as the Act states, "shall approximate as nearly as may be that which should be given by its parents."[18]

In 1902, a Children's Court was established in Manhattan (New York County); this became the first county in the country to have a children's court housed in its own building, the former Department of Public Charities Building on Third Avenue and 11th Street (demolished). This court was a division of the Court of Special Sessions and was still required by law to treat children in the same manner as adults. In 1915, the Children's Court was established as a separate court and in the next year it occupied a new courthouse on East 22nd Street that had been begun several years earlier. The site on East 22nd Street was probably chosen because of its location near several social-service organizations that dealt with issues relating to children: the New York Society for the Prevention of Cruelty to Children, which maintained its headquarters in a building on Park Avenue South at East 23rd Street *(see page 29)*; the Children's Aid Society housed in the United Charities Building *(see page 30)*; and, most importantly, the Charity Organization Society (also located in the United Charities Building), which was instrumental in the organization of the Children's Court.

The Children's Court is an imposing Classical Revival structure faced with limestone. The design is characteristic of public buildings erected in the early decades of the 20th century. The four-story building has a high rusticated base, two-story Ionic columns, and a full attic. In 1937, a bridge was built connecting this building to the new courthouse erected to the west. In 1959, the building was converted for use by Baruch College; the exterior remains unchanged.

---

18. Quoted in Kahn, p. 16. (See page 39).

NO. 137 EAST 22ND STREET
Facade detail

NO. 137 EAST 22ND STREET
Entrance detail

GUSTAVUS ADOLPHUS SWEDISH LUTHERAN CHURCH

153

145

155
Parish House

GUSTAVUS ADOLPHUS SWEDISH LUTHERAN CHURCH
No. 153 East 22nd Street, looking northwest, showing the adjacent church Parish House

145 East 22nd Street
Architect: George G. Miller
Date: 1939-40

THIS SYMMETRICALLY MASSED Colonial Revival apartment house is divided into two sections, each with an unusual pedimented roofline. At street level the sections are joined together by the entranceway with its handsome Colonial-inspired enframement with broken segmental-arched pediment and its doors crowned by a leaded transom. The red brick building was planned to house 47 families on six floors.

Gustavus Adolphus Swedish Lutheran Church
153 East 22nd Street
Architect: J.C. Cady & Co.
Date: 1887

J. C. CADY was the most talented architect in late-19th-century New York specializing in the design of Protestant (non-Episcopalian) churches. Cady worked extensively for Presbyterian and Methodist organizations, but was also responsible for buildings erected by other Protestant congregations including this Swedish Lutheran church designed using the Romanesque forms that he favored. Cady's design is superbly adapted to the Lutheran church's midblock site. A bold stone tower capped by a pyramidal roof rises along the streetline, attracting the atten-

tion of people walking along Lexington and Third avenues. The eye is then drawn downward to the deep round-arched, pedimented entry portal that leads into the sanctuary. The Gustavus Adolphus Church, named for King Gustavus Adolphus of Sweden, was established in 1865.

155 East 22nd Street
    (now Parish House of the Gustavus Adolphus Swedish
    Lutheran Church)
Architect: DeLemos & Cordes
Date: 1889

WITH ONE APARTMENT on each of its five floors, this Queen Anne style building is a fine example of the early apartment houses erected in the Gramercy Park area. The well-modulated facade has a rock-faced stone base that blends well with the neighboring church begun two years earlier. The upper floors are brick articulated by a variety of window arrangements and crowned by a projecting iron cornice. The facade is enlivened by the use of a two-story angled metal bay, iron tie rods, and a band of terra-cotta ornament. In 1947, the building became the Parish House of the Gustavus Adolphus Swedish Lutheran Church, and the two buildings received an internal connection.[19]

19. Early in the 1950s, an apartment in this building was repainted with a color scheme chosen by the great French architect Le Corbusier; see Stephen Garmey, *Gramercy Park: An Illustrated History of a New York Neighborhood* (New York: Balsam Press, 1984), p. 174

Gustavus Adolphus Swedish Lutheran Church
Rose window

EAST 22ND STREET, SOUTH SIDE, BETWEEN LEXINGTON AND THIRD AVENUES

140 EAST 22ND STREET (*Not shown*)

THIS MODERN APARTMENT house does not contribute to the character of the proposed extension to the Gramercy Park Historic District.

LEXINGTON
144 East 22nd Street
Architect: Sass & Smallheiser
Date: 1901

PRIOR TO THE PASSAGE of the 1901 Tenement House Act, the firm of Sass & Smallheiser was responsible for the design of a significant number of old law tenements, many located on the Lower East Side. The six-story apartment house at 144 East 22nd Street, planned almost immediately after the 1901 law went into effect, is a very early example of a new law apartment house. The Beaux-Arts brick building with rusticated limestone base and extensive terracotta trim was planned to house 29 middle-class families, four on the first floor and five on each of the upper floors.

MISS E.L. BREESE CARRIAGE HOUSE
150 East 22nd Street
Architect: Sidney V. Stratton
Date: 1893

SEVERAL STABLE and carriage-house structures once stood on this block of East 22nd Street, but only this small Neo-Flemish example survives. Built for Miss E.L. Breese by the socially well-connected architect Sidney V. Stratton, the building is a fine example of the private carriage houses that were erected in the late 19th century by some of New York's wealthiest citizens. This is the most substantial carriage house standing in the Gramercy Park neighborhood. The building is constructed of gold Roman brick with a white limestone base and trim and contains interesting overscaled voussoirs above the vehicular entrance, an unusual recessed blind arch encompassing the three second-floor windows, and a simple stepped pediment. By the 1920s, the building had been converted for use as a bakery; it is now a private residence.

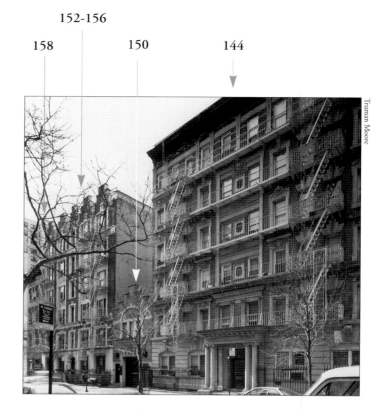

158   152-156   150   144

NOS. 144-158 EAST 22ND STREET
(right to left) looking southeast

MISS E.L. BREESE CARRIAGE HOUSE
No. 150 East 22nd Street

GRAMERCY COURT
152-156 East 22nd Street
Architect: Bernstein & Bernstein
Date: 1907

THIS RATHER UNUSUAL six-story structure was planned to house 32 families. Stylistically, the building is a rather whimsical amalgam of various forms. The symmetrically massed structure has a limestone base with a central Neo-Gothic entrance. The upper facade is clad in brick laid in Colonial Revival-inspired Flemish bond with burned headers. There is extensive terra-cotta detail on the upper stories, including ornate Renaissance spandrel panels and, below the third-floor windows, fanciful heads. Perhaps taking their cue for the design from the adjacent Breese Carriage House, Bernstein & Bernstein crowned this apartment building with an unusual row of five stepped gables.

158 EAST 22ND STREET
Architect: unknown
Date: unknown

THIS SIMPLE BRICK building was originally a four-story apartment building with a shop on the ground floor. The shop has been removed and a fifth-floor penthouse added. Of note on the facade are the brick window lintels and the galvanized-iron cornice.

NOS. 152-158 EAST 22ND STREET
(right to left), looking southwest

THIRD AVENUE

214   216   218

NOS. 214-18 THIRD AVENUE
Midblock between East 18th and 19th streets

THIRD AVENUE

THIRD AVENUE, WEST SIDE, BETWEEN EAST 18TH AND EAST 22ND STREETS

EAST
20TH STREET   244   246   248   250

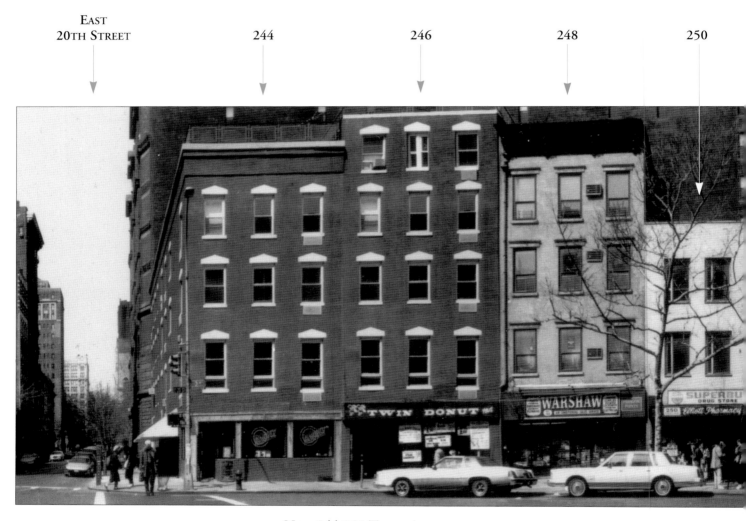

NOS. 244-258 THIRD AVENUE
Between East 20th and 21st streets

THREE OF THE blockfronts on the west side of Third Avenue between 18th Street and 22nd Street retain buildings that are a part of the original development of the Gramercy Park area. While the Gramercy Park frontages and the side streets in the area were initially built up primarily with single-family rowhouses, Third Avenue became the neighborhood's major commercial street. This avenue was developed almost entirely with three- and four-story brick buildings, each of which had a store on the ground floor and one or more living units above. In some cases the building was owned by the shopkeeper (as is still the case with several of the buildings today), with his or her family living above. Examples include Nos. **254** and **256** (c.1846), originally owned and occupied by

Barry Pribula

confectioner Frederick Thomas and butcher Joseph P. Flynn, respectively. In other instances, the buildings were owned by investors and leased to commercial and residential tenants.

The 17 extant early buildings date from the 1830s through the 1840s (two buildings within the boundaries — Nos. **250** and **252** — are not of historic interest). The trio of three-story structures at Nos. **214-218** Third Avenue between East 18th and 19th streets survive from an initial row of five erected in 1838. The blockfront between East 20th and 21st streets includes Nos. **244** and **246**, built c.1837 (No. **244** served as the Homeopathic

266   268   270   272   274

NOS. 266-280 THIRD AVENUE
Between East 21st and 22nd streets

Medical College for many years); No. **248** from 1840-41; the well-preserved four-story structures at Nos. **254** and **256**, from c.1846; and the two-story building at No. **258** that may date from as early as 1832, making it the oldest building in the area and the earliest surviving building erected by Gramercy Park's developer Samuel B. Ruggles. Between East 21st and 22nd streets are eight early buildings: three exceptionally narrow structures at Nos. **266-270**, dating from 1847, and five buildings, at Nos. **272-280**, erected in 1844-45. All are brick and display simple Greek Revival and Italianate features. These buildings are rare survivors on an avenue that has undergone major redevelopment since the 1950s.

276   278   280   EAST
                                       22ND STREET

Barry Pribula

EAST 19TH STREET

105   109   111   113   115   117

NOS. 105-117 EAST 19TH STREET, in 1992
Looking northwest, including a part of the National Arts Club on the right

105 EAST 19TH STREET
Architect: Neville & Bagge
Date: 1896

THE PROLIFIC ARCHITECTURAL firm of Neville & Bagge designed this carefully balanced six-story Neo-Renaissance apartment building with two eight-room apartments per floor. The building has a rusticated limestone base, brick upper floors trimmed with terra cotta, and a crowning metal cornice.

109 EAST 19TH STREET
Architect: unknown
Date: c.1858

THIS LARGE FOUR-STORY Anglo-Italianate brownstone-fronted rowhouse was one of several in the neighborhood erected by banker Elihu Townsend. The property was sold to James Hyslop, a prominent physician, who lived here until 1904. The building continued to house doctors after Hyslop sold the property. In 1908, a Dr. DeFaulk commissioned a one-story rear addition from Herts

50

& Tallant, an architectural firm with offices at 113 East 19th Street *(see below)*, and in 1932 Dr. David Schulman had the upper floors converted into six apartments. In 1985 Nicholas Pileggi wrote the novel *Wise Guy — Life in a Mafia Family* while living in this building; in the early 1990s, Pileggi and Martin Scorsese wrote the screenplay here for the movie adaptation, retitled *Goodfellas*. The house retains its original round-arched ground-floor openings (part of an arcade of arched windows running along the north side of this street) and original entrance doors, iron railings, parlor-floor casement windows, and deep cornice supported by paired brackets.

111 AND 113 EAST 19TH STREET
Architect: unknown
Date: c.1855

THIS PAIR OF narrow four-story Anglo-Italianate houses was built by Judge Thomas J. Oakley, who lived in the house at 12 Gramercy Park South that backed onto these 19th Street lots. Judge Oakley retained ownership of No. 111 until 1864; in 1908, No. 113 was acquired by Oakley's daughter and son-in-law, Matilda and William Rhinelander, in a foreclosure sale (they had purchased No. 111 in 1898). The houses retain such original features as their ground-floor arcade, segmental-arched windows, and wooden cornices. Between 1906 and 1911, No. 113 served as the offices of the prominent architectural firm of Herts & Tallant, best known for the design of such theaters as the New Amsterdam, Lyceum, and Brooklyn Academy of Music; during these years the building was also Henry Herts' home. The interior details of the house are said to reflect the taste of these architects.[20]

115 AND 117 EAST 19TH STREET
Architect: unknown
Date: c.1853

SLIGHTLY EARLIER in date than the pair to the west, these two narrow four-story Anglo-Italianate brownstone-fronted houses are crowned by a mansard roof (possibly an addition from the 1860s) and retain some of their original wooden window sash and iron railings.

---

20. Quoted in Garmey, p. 172 (See page 43).

NOS. 105-111 EAST 19TH STREET, c. 1940
Looking northwest

NO. 105 EAST 19TH STREET
Detail of entrance

IRT SUBSTATION
NO. 108 EAST 19TH STREET

INTERBOROUGH RAPID TRANSIT COMPANY SUBSTATION
108 East 19th Street
Architect: John Van Vleck and Paul C. Hunter
Date: 1902-04

THIS HANDSOME Renaissance-inspired powerhouse was built as part of the initial phase of construction on the Interborough Rapid Transit (IRT) subway. After many years of planning and discussion, work finally began on the construction of this, New York's first subway line, in 1899. Electricity to run the system was generated at an enormous power plant located on the block bounded by Eleventh and Twelfth avenues and West 58th and 59th streets. The power plant was planned to generate alternating current from the burning of coal. This current was directed to eight substations located along the route of the subway line, where it was converted into direct current. The current then flowed into the third rail placed alongside the subway tracks.[21]

The East 19th Street building is one of the eight original power substations. Unlike the main generating plant which was designed by one of the most prominent architectural firms of the era, the substations were designed by members of the IRT's own staff.[22]

The IRT was one of the most important public-works projects ever undertaken in New York. As such, the design of the system's stations, power plants, and other buildings was of great importance, and they were all designed to be architecturally distinguished. In fact, the city contract that permitted the Interborough Rapid Transit Company to build the subway included the following provision:

> The railway and its equipment as contemplated by the contract constitute a great public work. All parts of the structure where exposed to public sight shall therefore be designed, constructed, and maintained with a view to the beauty of their appearance, as well as to their efficiency.[23]

The East 19th Street substation is an eclectic structure. It is massed in a manner reminiscent of an Italian Renaissance palazzo and it is ornamented with French Beaux-Arts details such as cartouches and brackets hung with garlands. In addition, the upper story is faced with brick laid in a Georgian-inspired Flemish-bond pattern with burned headers. The four-story building is faced with fine materials; it has a granite base, limestone midsection, and the brick upper story, and contains iron window bays and terra-cotta detail. No longer used as a power station, the building was cleaned in 1990-91 and is presently vacant.

21. See *The New York Subway: Its Construction and Equipment* (New York: Interborough Rapid Transit, 1904).

22. The building permit for this structure lists the architect as John Van Vleck and Paul C. Hunter. The application was submitted on September 30, 1902. On that day Van Vleck and Hunter applied for two other powerhouses, on 148th Street and at City Hall Place. In the next month two other applications were submitted, for substations on West 96th Street and West 53rd Street. Only Paul Hunter is listed as the architect for these two buildings. All of the powerhouse designs are virtually identical.

23. Ibid, p. 15.

Window bay detail

122   120   118 116 112-114 108

NOS. 108-122 EAST 19TH STREET (right to left)
Looking southwest from Irving Place

112-114 EAST 19TH STREET
Architect: Charles E. Birge
Date: 1913-14

THE PRESENCE OF this simple 12-story brick, limestone, and terra-cotta loft building on what is basically a residential street is indicative of the eastward migration of industrial lofts that occurred in the area between 14th and 23rd streets in the early years of the 20th century.

116 EAST 19TH STREET
Architect: unknown; alteration, Harris V. Hartman
Date: c.1851; alteration, 1920-21

THE ALTERATION OF the facade of the brownstone rowhouse at 116 East 19th Street occurred in 1920-21 during the period when such redesign projects were extremely common in the Gramercy Park area. The new facade is a simple brick design highlighted by iron balconies and a sloping roof that was probably originally clad in Spanish tile. At the time the new streetfront was constructed, the interior was converted for use as offices and residences.

118 EAST 19TH STREET
Architect: unknown; alteration, Elias K. Herzog
Date: c.1851; alteration, 1944

IN 1944, the original streetfront of this rowhouse was removed and a new front wall was erected at the lot line. The new facade is a simple brick design with modest brick and stone highlights.

120 EAST 19TH STREET
Architect: unknown
Date: c.1853

WITH THE EXCEPTION of the loss of the stoop in 1923, this four-story brownstone-fronted Italianate rowhouse remains substantially as built and is representative of the thousands of similar houses that once lined the streets of Gramercy Park and adjoining neighborhoods. Of note are the heavy window enframements and the wooden cornice supported by curving brackets. In about 1913, muckraker Ida Tarbell, famous for her two-volume exposé of the Standard Oil Company, rented a small apartment in this building, where she lived until 1940.[24]

NO. 122 EAST 19TH STREET

122 EAST 19TH STREET
(aka 73-77 Irving Place)
Architect: unknown; alteration, Thain & Thain
Date: c.1853; alteration, 1908

THE HISTORY OF this Italianate rowhouse reflects the change that occurred on Irving Place as it evolved from a residential street to a street of mixed residential/commercial character. The house, which had its facade facing onto East 19th Street (now painted red), is a typical Italianate brownstone, with original wooden window sash and cornice intact. The Irving Place elevation is brick with modest brownstone trim. In 1908, the architectural firm of Thain & Thain was commissioned to remove the basement and first-floor walls, move the entrance to Irving Place, and build a two-story storefront with cast-iron columns, steel girders, and glass show windows. This 1908 alteration appears to have survived largely intact.

24. Kathleen Brady, *Ida Tarbell, Portrait of a Muckraker* (New York: Seaview/Putnam, 1984), pp. 205, 253-254.

Irving Place

65   67 - 69   71   73-77
(aka No. 122
East 19th
Street)

Truman Moore

Irving Place, in 1992
West side between 18th and 19th streets

IRVING PLACE
West side between 18th and 19th streets, March 1909

65 AND 71 IRVING PLACE
Architect: unknown
Date: c.1846

67-69 IRVING PLACE
Architect: Charles Volz
Date: 1910

NOS. **65** AND **71** Irving Place are two survivors from a row of four late Greek Revival houses that once also included Nos. **67** and **69** Irving Place. The facades of these simple but well-proportioned brick buildings are articulated by crisp rectilinear openings that become smaller on each successive floor. At the rooflines are projecting cornices. At No. **65**, the stoop was removed and the first floor and basement converted for commercial use in 1914 by architect Harrison G. Wiseman. No. **71** retains much of its original form, including its stoop. In the early 20th century the house was converted into furnished rooms. Residents included George Axelrod, author of the Broadway hit *The Seven Year Itch*, and the prominent Socialist, Norman Thomas.

CHARLES VOLZ'S 12-story loft with limestone base and terra-cotta-clad upper floors towers over the flanking pre-Civil War rowhouses. The building is a reflection of the commercialization of the street in the early 20th century, a development that can also be seen in the contemporaneous commercial alterations of several of the nearby rowhouses.

No. 81 Irving Place
Looking northwest

81 IRVING PLACE
Architect: George Pelham
Date: 1929-30

FOR THIS 14-story apartment house, architect George Pelham, one of New York's most active apartment-house designers, exploited the requirements of the zoning law to create an exuberant design with dramatic set-backs and a striking rooftop pavilion surrounding the water tower. The building, planned with 107 small apartments, is faced with brick, often laid in intricate patterns to add excitement to the facades. The building is ornamented with beige terra-cotta detail of a very high quality. Terra-cotta features include columns, balconies, and gargoyles embellished with animal heads, monsters, and other fanciful detail.

Terra-cotta balcony

Terra-cotta window details

Terra-cotta detail

LATE-19TH-CENTURY PHOTO SHOWING SOUTHWEST CORNER OF IRVING PLACE AND 17TH STREET
(See pages 64-65)

PART TWO
PROPOSED
17TH STREET/IRVING PLACE
HISTORIC DISTRICT

IRVING PLACE

EAST 18TH STREET

EAST 17TH STREET

GRAMERCY AREA
HISTORIC PRESERVATION STUDY

EXISTING DISTRICT (DESIGNATED 1966)

HISTORIC DISTRICT EXTENSION
(DESIGNATED 1988)

PROPOSED NEW DISTRICT

EXISTING INDIVIDUAL LANDMARK

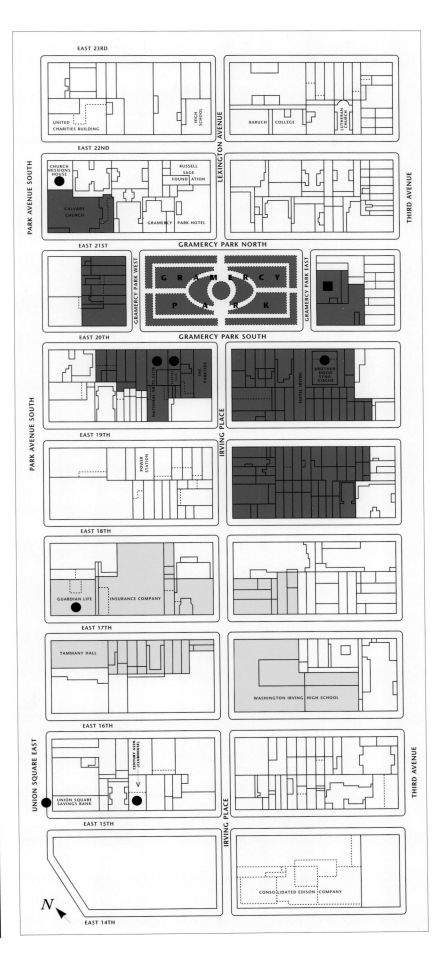

THE PROPOSED **17th Street/Irving Place Historic District** consists of buildings facing onto Irving Place as well as buildings on East 17th and East 18th streets, to the east and west of Irving Place. Within the district ia a wide variety of buildings reflecting the complex developmental history of the Gramercy Park neighborhood. There are many single-family rowhouses from the 1840s and 1850s, typical of the early development period in the neighborhood. Beginning in the 1870s, the Gramercy Park area became one of the first sections of New York City to experience the construction of apartment houses planned for the middle class. Several of these relatively modest apartment houses, some with finely designed facades, survive in the proposed district. In addition, the proposed historic district contains several important institutional buildings, notably Washington Irving High School and Tammany Hall, and the commercial Germania Life Insurance Company Building, now the Guardian Life Insurance Company Building, with its handsome International style annex. The largest cluster of buildings in the proposed historic district lines, the south side of East 17th Street between Union Square East and Irving Place. This is one of the most unusual blocks in New York, a block that the *New York Times* referred to in 1989 as "a minor urban masterpiece."[25] The buildings on this street were erected over a period of more than half a century; yet the block has an extraordinary charm and cohesion that are rare in New York City. Since this proposed district is a single unit that is physically independent of the designated Gramercy Park Historic District and is considerably smaller than the proposed extensions to that district, the buildings in this area are discussed in a single text that highlights its cohesive character and historical development.

The oldest buildings in the proposed historic district are Greek Revival rowhouses dating from the 1840s. The earliest are **Nos. 54 and 56 Irving Place,** erected in 1840-41. These two brick rowhouses, located on the east side of Irving Place between East 17th and East 18th streets, are survivors from a row of six that was among the earliest erected in the Gramercy Park area. They are two of the finest Greek Revival buildings in the neighborhood, with their massive templelike brownstone entrance enframements, high stoops, simple stone window lintels and sills, and, at No. 56, wrought- and cast-iron stoop railings and denticulated cornice. No. 54 was modernized, probably in 1879, by the addition of a handsome oriel window (once capped by an iron cresting) and massive cornice, both in the Neo-Grec style.

Each of these houses was originally a single-family residence, but as the character of the Gramercy Park neighborhood changed in the early 20th century, rowhouse occupancy changed throughout the area. For some years, No. 54 was occupied by the Ingersoll Club, one of many private clubs that moved to the streets on or near Gramercy Park. By the 1920s, No. 56 had become a boarding house. A major change in use occurred in 1921 when No. 54 was converted into the Cooperative Cafeteria; in 1924 the cafeteria expanded into No. 56.

The **Cooperative Cafeteria** was a project of the Consumers' Co-operative Services of New York City (CCS), one of several cooperative

NOS. 54-56 IRVING PLACE, IN 1938

25. Christopher Gray, "10 Houses With Collective Charm," *New York Times*, October 8, 1989, sec. 10, p. 6.

organizations founded in New York City shortly after World War I that sought to provide working people with quality services (restaurants, shops, housing, etc.) at reasonable prices. CCS was organized by a group of middle-class American-born individuals (most cooperative ventures were founded by immigrants) who opened a cafeteria on East 25th Street in 1919 and soon began selling shares in the business to their patrons. The venture was so successful that in 1921 CCS expanded to Irving Place, and eventually opened two other branches in Lower Manhattan. The success of the cafeterias led the CCS to open cooperative bakeries, food shops, a laundry (unsuccessful), a circulating library, and a credit union; in 1930 the organization erected a non-profit cooperative apartment building at 433 West 21st Street. CCS soon become the largest cooperative venture in the eastern United States, in both membership and sales.[26]

The Irving Place cafeteria had its kitchen in the basement, with the dining rooms in the basement and first story. Upper stories contained the cooperative's central offices, staff living quarters, and a spare guest room. A description of the CCS cafeterias, published in 1925, reports that "frank, cheerful simplicity and worth are the keynotes in the decorations of the establishments, in the conduct of the employees, as well as in the preparation of the dishes."[27] The cafeteria remained open for many years, finally being replaced by a succession of other commercial establishments. Restoration work was undertaken on the two rowhouses in 1992-93.

Nos. 54-56 Irving Place, in 1993

Another Greek Revival house can be seen at **120 East 17th Street.** Probably dating from the mid-1840s, the facade of this building remains largely intact, with original iron stoop railings, simple wooden cornice and stone window lintels and sills, and multi-paned wooden windows.

26. C. Long, "Consumers Cooperative Services," *Cooperation 16* (March 1930), p. 42.
27. "Co-operative Restaurants," *Cooperation 11* (November 1925), p. 203.

47   49

SOUTHWEST CORNER OF IRVING PLACE AND 17TH STREET, in 1909
The Westminster Hotel, once located to the left, had been demolished and its present-day
replacement not yet built when this photograph was taken

Perhaps the most interesting of the early houses in this area are **47 and 49 Irving Place** (c.1844), a pair of simple three-story and basement brick rowhouses. Architecturally, 49 Irving Place is among the outstanding houses in the Gramercy Park area. Although many houses erected in the 1840s survive in New York City, this dwelling is special for its ornamental detail. Of note are the stoop railing and extraordinary cast-iron veranda at the entrance on 17th Street, the adjacent three-sided oriel, and the cast-iron balcony on Irving Place with its wooden hood. This ornament may be original, or may date from an alteration, probably in the 1850s. No. 47 Irving Place also retains its original stoop ironwork, while the four-story rear extension of No. 49, dating from the 1850s or 1860s, has a large oriel and unusual dormer (similar dormers have been removed from No. 49).[28]

NO. 49 IRVING PLACE
Entrance stoop ironwork

28. The rear extension of 49 Irving Place is not original. Tax-assessment records list a house measuring 19′ x 38′ on a lot of 19′ x 60′ through 1885. In 1886 the records note that the lot is "covered." This conflicts with records on city atlases. The extension does not appear on the Dripps atlas of 1867, but it does appear on the Perris atlas of 1868.

SOUTHWEST CORNER OF IRVING PLACE AND 17TH STREET, in 1992

Great historic significance is often attached to the house at 49 Irving Place; it is claimed that the great American author Washington Irving once lived here. It is, however, unlikely that Washington Irving ever crossed the threshold of this house. Washington Irving's nephew, Edgar Irving, bought 120 East 17th Street in 1851. It is quite possible that Washington Irving visited Edgar and his family in that house.[29] The legend of Irving's association with 49 Irving Place has a long pedigree, dating back to the 19th century, and it has been sanctified by the presence of a bronze plaque installed in 1934.[30] An investigation of the creation of the Irving legend might provide interesting insights into the author's importance as an American icon. No. 49 Irving Place was, however, indisputably the home of Elsie de Wolfe, America's first professional interior decorator, and her companion Elisabeth Marbury, from 1892 to 1912; during this period they rented the house, running a famous salon here. No. 49 was considered for landmark designation by the Landmarks Preservation Commission in 1966, but no action was taken. No. 47 is of historical interest as the site where Oscar Wilde lodged in 1883 while his unsuccessful play *Vera* was in rehearsal at the nearby Union Square Theater.[31]

29. Much of the information concerning 120 East 17th Street and 49 Irving Place was located by Stephen Garmey. An article published in the *New York Times* on June 12, 1911, reports that Edgar Irving's son-in-law, Charles R. Huntington, who lived at 120 East 17th Street with his wife, Amanda Irving Huntington, categorically denied that Washington Irving had ever visited 49 Irving Place. The article notes that other Irving relatives corroborated Huntington's report. Christopher Gray, in his "Why the Legend of Irving Is but a Myth," *New York Times*, March 3, 1994, sec. 10, p. 6, also debunks the story.

30. The Irving connection has been cited many times. For example, the *New York Sun* reported on August 13, 1927, that George Haven Putnam, son of the founder of the Putnam publishing house, "recalled his having gone to Irving House many times as a boy to receive from the hands of Washington Irving communications addressed to his father." William Wash Williams wrote in his biography of his friend O. Henry that "at the corner of Seventeenth and the Place I brought him [O. Henry] to a stop before the little yellow house, long accepted as the old city home of Washington Irving. Some contention or controversy has arisen since as to whether Irving really lived in that house or the one next to it." William Wash Williams, *The Quiet Lodger of Irving Place* (New York: E.P. Dutton, 1936), pp. 48-49. In addition, Arthur Bartlett Maurice wrote in *The New York of the Novelists* (New York: Dodd, Mead & Co., 1915, p. 5) that this was Irving's last New York home and that he wrote portions of several books here.

31. Richard Ellmann, *Oscar Wilde* (New York: Knopf, 1988), pp. 205-06, 241-43. Also, see Hesketh Pearson, *Oscar Wilde: His Life and Wit* (New York: Harper & Brothers, 1946), p. 68. The latter also cites (p. 68) Wilde's lodging at 47 Irving Place as having been "next door to the house once occupied by Washington Irving."

49 IRVING PLACE   120   118   116

SOUTH SIDE OF 17TH STREET BETWEEN Irving Place and Union Square East. A block that the *New York Times* in 1989 called "a minor urban masterpiece." (Composite photograph)

Chronologically, the last Greek Revival rowhouse in the proposed district is **104 East 17th Street,** dating from c.1848. This brick house retains its original brownstone entrance enframement and iron stoop railing. The galvanized-iron cornice and window lintels are, however, in the Renaissance Revival style and were probably added in the early 20th century.

Rowhouse construction in the area south of Gramercy Park and north of 14th Street continued in the 1850s; however, the style of choice for developers changed from the Greek Revival to the Italianate. Within the proposed 17th Street/Irving Place Historic District are five Italianate rowhouses. Four of the Italianate dwellings, all dating from c.1854, are located on East 17th Street between Union Square East and Irving Place — the brick residence at **106 East 17th Street,** the pair of brownstone-fronted houses at **108 and 110 East 17th Street**, and the individual brownstone at **116 East 17th Street.** No. 106, the simplest of the houses, had its stoop removed in 1917 when it was converted into studio apartments.[32] **Nos. 108 and**

112   110   108   106   104

Truman Moore

110 are especially grand dwellings. Each is four stories tall above a raised basement and is capped by a bracketed cornice. Still extant at No. 110 is a massive foliate doorway lintel, an elegant cast-iron parlor-floor balcony, and a pair of newel posts. In 1918-19, the stoop was removed from No. 108 and it was converted from a one-family residence into non-housekeeping apartments (i.e., apartments without kitchens).[33]

---

32. The architect for this conversion was Herbert Lucas, the designer of 24 Gramercy Park South (located in the designated historic district) and 1 Lexington Avenue.

33. The Certificate of Occupancy for the building refers to these units as "bachelor apartments." There were four of these units per floor. The prestigious firm of Renwick, Aspinwall & Tucker was responsible for this alteration.

118

Barry Pribula

118 East 18th Street
Between Irving Place and Park Avenue South

The fifth Italianate house is the relatively late example of the style located at **118 East 18th Street.** This four-story and raised basement brownstone-front house is the only survivor of the dwellings that once lined this block. It was erected as an individual building, not part of a row, and was the last house built on this block. The building was designed in 1868 by prominent architect Stephen Decatur Hatch and was commissioned by Henry T. Ingalls. Ingalls was an importer of ivory, ebony, shell, and other tropical goods. He moved to 18th Street from 102 East 17th Street (now the site of Tammany Hall; *(see page 78)*. The facade, restored in the early 1990s, displays such typical Italianate features as a segmental-arched entrance (the stoop is missing), sculptural window enframements, and rusticated base. The stylized brackets of the galvanized-iron cornice hint at the fact that this is a late Italianate building.

Also dating from the 1850s is **121 East 17th Street**, a former carriage house erected in c.1854 for J.O. Ward, who lived at 51 Irving Place. Although this simple Early Romanesque Revival brick building has undergone many changes in use (carriage house, garage, restaurant, office, and residence), it still retains much of its original character. The Landmarks Preservation Commission held a public hearing on the designation of this building in 1970, but no action was taken. (*See opposite page and page 6*).

GUARDIAN LIFE
INSURANCE COMPANY
EXTENSION   119   121   53 IRVING PLACE

NORTH SIDE OF 17TH STREET, in 1993
Between Irving Place and Park Avenue
South, showing Guardian Life
Insurance Company Extension at the
left (see page 79)

119   121

NORTH SIDE OF 17TH STREET, in 1938
Between Irving Place and Park Avenue South (see page 6)

Truman Moore

No. 129 East 17th Street
Thought to be New York's oldest intact apartment house

By the 1870s, the Gramercy Park neighborhood was almost entirely built up with rowhouses; construction, however, did not cease in the area. Instead of single-family homes, apartment houses began to appear, either on vacant sites or in place of early homes that were demolished. Among these were some of the earliest middle-class apartment houses erected in New York City. In fact, the five-story building at **129 East 17th Street**, designed by Napoleon Le Brun in 1878 and completed in 1879, is thought to be the city's oldest intact apartment house.[34] Although Richard Morris Hunt's now-demolished Stuyvesant Apartments, the first middle-class apartment house in the city, had opened on East 18th Street in 1870, only a few similar buildings were erected in the following years. This was partly due to the fact that apartment-house living was not immediately accepted by the middle class and partly to the real-estate depression caused by the Panic of 1873. The East 17th Street building was one of the first apartment houses erected when construction resumed in the late 1870s as the effects of the panic subsided. The building was planned to house five families behind a stylish Gothic Revival brick and brownstone facade.

Architect Napoleon Le Brun was already a well-known designer in New York when he received this commission. He had moved to New York in 1864 from Philadelphia, where he had designed the Academy of Music and the Cathedral of SS. Peter and Paul. In New York, he had designed the Masonic Temple on West 23rd Street (demolished), St. John the Baptist R.C. Church on West 30th Street, and other buildings. Later, in association with his sons, Le Brun designed many of the city's firehouses, as well as the Metropolitan Life Insurance Company's landmarked tower on Madison Square.

In 1890, two rowhouses on East 17th Street were demolished and replaced by the **Fanwood** at **112 East 17th Street**, a six-story Romanesque Revival apartment house planned for 12 families (two per floor). The Fanwood was one of the earliest works of George Pelham, who is first listed as an architect in New York City directories in the year that the Fanwood was designed.[35] This building has an unusual brownstone base with projecting rock-faced bands and a massive entrance portico. The upper facade is brick with brownstone trim and contains a three-story arcade rising from the third to the fifth floor. The cornice dates from 1898 when an alteration permit called for the removal of the front coping and the addition of a galvanized-iron cornice. This explains why the cornice has more of a Renaissance character than has the remainder of the building.

34. Christopher Gray, "The 'Oldest' Apartment House," *New York Times*, July 9, 1990, sec. 10, p. 6.

35. Dennis Steadman Francis, *Architects in Practice:New York City 1840-1900* , p. 60 (New York: Committee for the Preservation of Architectural Records, 1980). Pelham also designed 81 Irving Place.

NO. 52 IRVING PLACE, in 1909

East side between 17th and 18th Streets, looking northeast, showing the original house at the northeast corner of 17th Street and the Huyler's Chocolate Factory at the corner of 18th Street

NO. 52 IRVING PLACE, in 1995

Showing six-story building originally designed as bachelor's flats

To the east of the Fanwood is the **Irving,** an apartment house located at **118 East 17th Street**. This narrow structure, designed in 1901 by Alfred E. Badt, has handsome Renaissance-inspired detail. The building is of note because it was designed almost immediately after the passage of the 1901 Tenement House Act, which sought to abolish multiple dwellings on narrow lots since these buildings generally filled their entire site and did not allow adequate light and air to reach most rooms. Despite its narrow width, the plan was praised by Lawrence Veiller, one of the leading tenement-reform advocates. Veiller analyzed the layout, commenting that "all rooms are of a good size and are well lighted and ventilated....Although the lot is only 20 feet wide and 81 feet deep, the architect has been able to get very good results for the particular type of flat desired by his client."[36]

The final multiple dwelling in the proposed district is located at **52 Irving Place** (aka 123 East 17th Street). This handsome Colonial Revival style red brick building with white stone trim and a projecting iron cornice was commissioned in 1912 by John S. Foster, who lived next door at 54 Irving Place. Designed by Charles C. Thain, this six-story building was planned with bachelor's apartments. Bachelor's flats were modest apartment houses erected to house single men in small but well-appointed suites that lacked kitchen facilities. In the early years of the 20th century, a number of these buildings appeared in the vicinity of Gramercy Park since the many clubs in the neighborhood provided a venue for meals and entertainment. No. 52 Irving Place originally had 18 apartments of from two to four rooms. In 1933, by which time buildings especially for bachelors had ceased to be popular, kitchens were added to the small suites.

36. "Two New Law Flats," *Real Estate Record and Builders Guide* 69 (February 8, 1902), p. 250.

WASHINGTON IRVING HIGH SCHOOL, in 1994

Besides the rowhouses and apartment buildings, the proposed historic district includes two institutional buildings and a single office building. The larger of the institutional buildings is **Washington Irving High School**, located at 40 Irving Place between East 16th and East 17th streets. This is a significant institution in the history of women's education in New York City. It is of additional importance for its exceptional Gothic-inspired public spaces and its extensive series of mural decorations (this interior is proposed for interior designation). The school that was to become Washington Irving was organized in 1902 as a branch of Wadleigh High School (at the time, the only girls' high school in Manhattan). Known initially as Girls' Technical High School, the institution was the idea of progressive educator William McAndrew, who believed that girls training for vocational or technical trades and those undertaking an academic curriculum should be educated together since they had much to teach each other.

The school proved to be extremely successful, with classes held in five different buildings. The increasing enrollment justified the erection of a new building planned specifically for the needs of the diverse female student body. Land was purchased on Irving Place, opposite the building reputed to be associated with Washington Irving, and the name of the institution was changed to honor that great American author. In 1908, Superintendent of School Buildings C.B.J. Snyder designed a seven-story brick, limestone, and terra-cotta structure with an imposing arched entrance, paired round-arched Florentine Renaissance windows on the seventh floor, a deep cornice, and a tiled hip roof. The building was to cost $600,000.[37] Two years later the proposed building was enlarged with the addition of another story and a flat roof that would be available for recreation. Since the cost was to remain the same, it became "necessary to re-design the exterior to simplify same by eliminating some of the stone and terra cotta treatment appearing in the earlier design."[38] Construction on the school began in 1911 and was completed in 1913.

37. This design is described and illustrated with elevations and plans in New York Art Commission, "Washington Irving High School (Girls' Technical School)," Submission 778, Series 359—AH.

38. Ibid., 359—I.

WASHINGTON IRVING HIGH SCHOOL, c. 1920
Irving Place, east side, between 16th and 17th Streets, showing original cornice, supported by cast-iron brackets, and roof trellises. Tracks of the 17th Street horse-drawn trolley are still in place.

The school's simple street elevations have a two-story limestone base, with the upper stories clad in gray brick trimmed with limestone and terra cotta. A cornice above the eighth floor is supported by wrought-iron brackets. The rooftop recreation area was originally marked by a trellis to "disguise more or less the necessary caging incidental to a roof playground."[39] This rooftop arrangement has been altered.

The planning of interior spaces at Washington Irving High School was extremely difficult since the school needed a wide variety of facilities for its extensive curriculum. An article on the school published in *The American Architect* in 1913 discusses this problem:

WASHINGTON IRVING HIGH SCHOOL, c. 1960
Main entrance

> The difficulty has been to provide a building that would combine within the walls of a single structure, all the various utilities that would be necessary to encompass such diversified educational features....In order to understand the complexity of the problem involved in the planning of this schoolhouse, it may be well to set down the principal departments of study that are provided. They

are;—Housekeeping, nursing, marketing, care of babies, laundering, embroidery, plain sewing, garment making, costume designing, drawing, illustrating, plain and fancy cooking, entertaining, sanitation, picture hanging, telephoning, dancing, stair-climbing, typewriting, bookkeeping, stenography, salesmanship, office management, bookbinding, cataloguing, commercial filing, printing, photography, gardening, newspaper writing, and in addition the usual high school branches, namely Latin, German, French, Spanish and Italian, singing, physics, chemistry, biology, mathematics, physiology and civics.[40]

All of these needs were to be accommodated in 94 classrooms. From its inauguration in February 1913, the school's enrollment far exceeded its capacity during normal hours. The Superintendent of Schools reported in 1913 that Principal William McAndrew devised "an ingenious arrangement, under which the building is kept open until late in the afternoon and each classroom is made to accommodate several sections at different hours of the day; the building now provides for

39. Ibid.
40. "The Washington Irving High School," *The American Architect 103* (March 19, 1913), pp. 146-148.

more than twice the number of students it was intended to house, yet each student receives a full day's schooling."[41] It was not until 1932 that design began for an addition to the school. Located on East 16th Street, the 12-story addition, completed in 1938, was designed by Superintendent of School Buildings Walter C. Martin. Since its opening, Washington Irving High School has had many graduates who went on to great success. Among the most famous have been Claudette Colbert, Sylvia Sidney, Bella Spewack, and Norma Kamali.

The exterior of the original building is extremely simple, lacking the ornate quality of some of Snyder's other early-20th-century high-school designs, such as the Collegiate Gothic Morris (1900-04) in The Bronx and Curtis (1902-04) on Staten Island and the Neo-Flemish DeWitt Clinton (1904-06) in Manhattan. The interior public spaces of Washington Irving High School, however, are among the most impressive in any New York City school and should be designated as an interior landmark. These consist of a two-story foyer with a mezzanine balcony, and a large skylit auditorium, all designed in Snyder's favorite Collegiate Gothic mode.

The foyer, with its massive fireplace inglenook and handsome woodwork, was planned as a homey environment where classes, such as sewing and embroidery, could be conducted.[42] As at many of the high schools erected in the first years of the century, murals were to be an important aspect of the interior decor. Apparently, the foyer and mezzanine were originally to contain a series of 20 murals depicting characters from various Washington Irving tales, including Rip Van

WASHINGTON IRVING HIGH SCHOOL
Foyer, showing original murals and two-story space with a mezzanine balcony

Winkle and the Headless Horseman.[43] Although these specific murals were never executed, the public spaces at Washngton Irving contain one of the most extensive art projects in a New York City public school, with four separate mural projects and sculpture contributed by two additional artists.

41. *Fifteenth Annual Report of the City Superintendent of Schools for the Year Ending July 31, 1913* (1913), p. 88.

42. Above the fireplace is carved the school's motto: "The fire of hospitality in the home and the glow of cordiality in the heart." This line comes from Washington Irving's *Bracebridge Hall*. The "homelike air" of the foyer is discussed in "Most Remarkable Girls' School in the World," *New York Times,* February 2, 1913, p. 10.

43. Ibid., p. 148.

WASHINGTON IRVING HIGH SCHOOL
Early photograph of foyer showing fireplace and murals in adjacent spaces.

FOYER FIREPLACE, in 1994
With original plaster bas-relief by Francis Taft Grimes

The high school's first series of murals was begun in 1915 when Mrs. E.H. Harriman announced that she would donate a cycle of 12 murals for the foyer walls, to be painted by Barry Faulkner. This gift was offered to the city through the Municipal Art Society. Faulkner was among the most prominent members of the second generation of American mural painters, working primarily in the second, third, and fourth decades of the 20th century. The Washington Irving murals were undertaken relatively early in Faulkner's career. Perhaps his most famous work in New York City is the mosaic mural at the Sixth Avenue entrance to the former RCA Building West, at Rockefeller Center; other murals were created for the Cunard Building at 25 Broadway and for the Oregon and New Hampshire state capitols. Installation began on the murals in 1917; the cycle was completed in 1921. The paintings include scenes from Irving's *Knickerbocker's History of New York City*, as well as maps, and panels displaying local flora and fauna.[44] This series of paintings is part of the Municipal Art Society's Adopt-A-Mural program, which seeks private grants for the restoration and maintenance of public artwork.[45]

WASHINGTON IRVING HIGH SCHOOL
1914 photograph of students sewing at foyer fireplace inglenook

Other works of art in the foyer are bronze tablets of Washington Irving and Abraham Lincoln, both by Victor D. Brenner, and a plaster bas-relief over the fireplace showing three women, the central figure reading a book. The panel·includes a quote from Irving's *The Legend of Sleepy Hollow*. This was the work of Francis Taft Grimes, a member of the Saint-Gaudens circle at the

44. The 12 scenes are *Indians in Manhattan, Henry Hudson Landing on the Island of Manhattan, The Pioneer Women, The Peach War, Picture Map of Peter Stuyvesant's Bouwerie Farm, The Kissing Bridge, Picture Map of Long Island, Manhattan, The Sound and the Connecticut Shore, The Path of the Fur Traders* (a map), *Peter Stuyvesant Landing His Army Against the Swedes in New Orange, Picture Map of New Amsterdam with the British Ships Under Captain Nichols, in the Bay, Demanding the Surrender of the Town*, and two flora and fauna scenes, each surrounding a ventilator with a metal grille in the form of a ship (the ships are the *Tiger*, one of the first trading vessels to arrive at Manhattan, and the *Unrest*, the first ship built on Manhattan).

45. Municipal Art Society, *Adopt-A-Mural* (New York: Municipal Art Society, 1991), pp. 36-37.

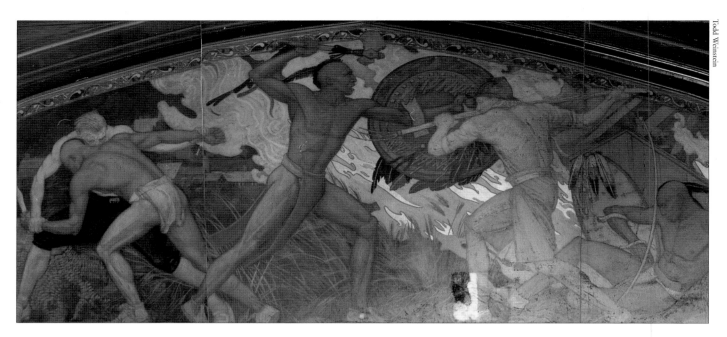

WASHINGTON IRVING HIGH SCHOOL (composite photograph)
Close-up of mural by Barry Faulkner: *The Peach War*

FOYER VIEW OF FAULKNER MURAL:
The Peach War

Cornish Colony in New Hampshire, who also created works for the Hall of Fame Terrace in The Bronx and Washington Cathedral.

The second series of murals donated to the school was presented in 1915 by a mural-painting committee of the Society of Beaux-Arts Architects. This is a series of scenes of New Amsterdam, painted by muralist and illustrator Robert Knight Ryland, for the auditorium. The initial plan called for several scenes on the rear wall of the auditorium, each divided by decorative panels with busts, plants and animals, and Indian objects. Additional decorative forms were to be painted on the side walls. At present, the only panel that is visible is one in the center of the rear wall that shows the Dutch and Indians trading.[46]

In the front of the auditorium are 12 narrow panels with female figures painted by J. Mortimer Lichtenauer in 1932. The six panels to the left of the stage, with their heads uplifted, represent idealism, inspiration, spirit, hope, vision, and aspiration. The corresponding group, with their heads down, represent botany, cooking, history, science, literature, and athletics. According to the artist, "though each panel has a single figure, a carefully considered rhythm of line and form will be noted throughout."[47]

---

46. Decorative elements that once flanked this scene have been overpainted. It is not clear if the other panels planned for the rear wall and the decorative panels for the side walls were ever executed.

47. Art Commission, No. 359—BQ.

WASHINGTON IRVING HIGH SCHOOL
Foyer view of mural by Barry Faulkner:
*Peter Stuyvesant Landing His Army Against the Swedes
in New Orange*

WASHINGTON IRVING HIGH SCHOOL
Henry Hudson Landing on the Island of Manhattan

Bust of Washington Irving
by Friedrich Beer

The final mural cycle in the main public areas is Salvatore Lascari's extensive two-story work on the stairs, running from the first to the third floor, depicting historic landmarks of New York.[48] This mural was originally planned in 1915, with architect Charles Stoughton listed as the artist, but it was not until 1934 that the scenes of old and new New York were actually begun. According to a painted plaque that is part of the completed work, it was a gift of the Municipal Art Society, with the design by Stoughton (the president of the society), and painting by Lascari. This mural, like others at the high school, is in dire need of restoration.

In addition to these works commissioned specifically for the high school, a bust of Washington Irving was placed in front of the building in 1935. The work of sculptor Friedrich Beer, the bronze had been commissioned in 1885 and was to be installed in Central Park. Controversy concerning the artistic merits of the piece led to its placement in Bryant Park. When the park was redesigned during the 1930s, the bust was removed and reinstalled on Irving Place, north of the main entrance to Washington Irving High School.[49]

---

48. There are additional murals, dating from the early 1940s, in the cafeteria located in the addition. These are the work of George and Mary McAndrew Stonehill and were a gift of the artists (Mrs. Stonehill was the daughter of the school's first principal, William McAndrew).

49. Margot Gayle and Michele Cohen, *The Art Commission and the Municipal Art Society Guide to Manhattan's Outdoor Sculpture* (New York: Prentice Hall Press, 1988), p. 98.

Nos. 100-102 East 17th Street
Former Tammany Hall

On the southeast corner of East 17th Street and Union Square East, at 100-102 East 17th Street, stands the second of the district's institutional buildings, **Tammany Hall,** once the headquarters of New York City's Democratic Party political machine. Late in 1927, the Society of Tammany sold its headquarters on East 14th Street and announced the construction of a new Tammany Hall. Plans for the new building were made public in January 1928.[50] The building, designed by Thompson, Holmes & Converse and Charles B. Meyers, was to be a Colonial Revival structure built of red Harvard brick with granite trim (limestone was later substituted). The *Real Estate Record* described the design as "a dignified architectural treatment, one of the chief motifs of which are the severe Colonial columns in the centers of the Union Square and the Seventeenth-street facades which recall the days of early American architecture."[51]

The Colonial Revival was undoubtedly chosen not only because it was reminiscent of the architecture of the early republic, but also because it symbolized the government established during that period. The Society of Tammany was attempting to associate itself with the ideals of early American democracy; in fact, the Union Square facade bears a striking resemblance to the original Federal Hall, where George Washington took the oath of office as the first President of the United States. By choosing the Colonial Revival style, with all that it symbolized, Tammany may have been attempting to create the image of a truly democratic force to counter the accusations that it was a corrupt political machine.

---

50. "Architects Picked for Tammany Hall," *New York Times,* January 18, 1928, p. 52; "New Tammany Hall Will Be Colonial in Design," *Real Estate Record and Builders Guide 121* (January 28, 1928), p. 7. The *Real Estate Record* article includes an elevation drawing. A slightly different elevation drawing, closer to the building as actually constructed, was illustrated in the Architectural League's *Yearbook* (1929), n.p.

51. "New Tammany Hall... ."

The building, as completed in 1929, included commercial space facing Union Square (originally occupied by a branch of the Manufacturers Trust Company), a public meeting hall on the east side of the first floor, offices for the Democratic County Committee, and a series of committee and meeting rooms. In 1943, the building was sold to the International Ladies Garment Workers Union; the main meeting hall, renamed Roosevelt Auditorium, became one of the most important centers for union activities in New York City. In 1984, the hall was renovated for use as an Off-Broadway theater.

The proposed historic district's one important office building complex is that of the **Guardian Life Insurance Company** (originally the **Germania Life Insurance Company**), at 50 Union Square East, with an extension at 105 East 17th Street. The company's 20-story skyscraper at the northeast corner of Union Square, with facades facing Park Avenue South and East 17th Street, is a designated individual landmark. The building was designed by D'Oench & Yost in 1910 and is best known for its enormous mansard roof crowned by an electric sign. The Germania Life Insurance Company was founded in 1860 and changed its name in 1918 in response to anti-German feelings generated by World War I. The building has an elegant three-story modern extension that is not part of its landmark designation. The addition, which stretches from East 17th Street through the block to East 18th Street, was designed by Skidmore, Owings & Merrill and built in 1959-63. The large plate-glass windows, aluminum spandrel panels set flush with the glass, and the projecting vertical mullions create a sophisticated, beautifully proportioned geometry that is representative of the finest International style design. The building has a lobby and offices on the first story, offices and a cafeteria on the second story, offices on the third story, and a rooftop terrace. In order to connect the addition to the original headquarters structure on the corner of Park Avenue South, the first two floors of the modern structure match the height of the headquarters' entrance hall; the third story of the addition lines up with the second story of the older building.

Stephen Garmey

NO. 105 EAST 17TH STREET SIDE OF GUARDIAN LIFE INSURANCE CO. EXTENSION, showing the geometric facade of windows and panels that reflect the houses across the street on the south side, and echo the general scale of windows and building heights.

Barry Pribula

GUARDIAN LIFE INSURANCE CO. EXTENSION

EAST 18TH STREET SIDE OF GUARDIAN LIFE INSURANCE CO. EXTENSION
Addition stretches through the block to East 17th Street
(see page 69)

Also within the boundaries of the proposed historic district are two non-contributing buildings: **No. 119 East 17th Street,** a seriously altered rowhouse, and the modern apartment house at **53 Irving Place**. building replaces three rowhouses, including one, at 55 Irving Place, where short-story writer O. Henry rented a room from 1902-1910.

NOS. 132-138 EAST 16TH STREET *(right to left)*
No. 136, showing 1889 cast-iron facade elements by Herter Brothers, is one of the most extraordinary buildings in the
Gramercy Park neighborhood. *(See page 86)*

PART THREE
PROPOSED INDIVIDUAL
LANDMARK BUILDINGS

THIRD AVENUE

EAST 17TH STREET

EAST 16TH STREET

EAST 15TH STREET

IRVING PLACE

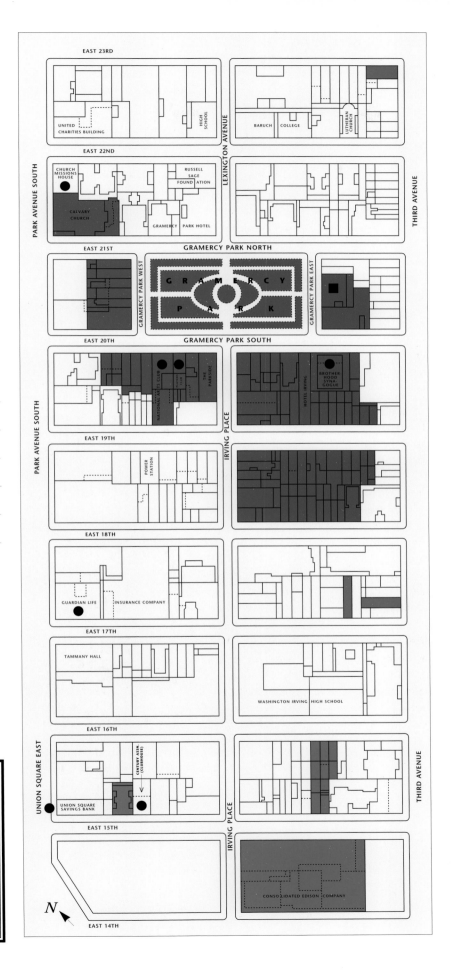

GRAMERCY AREA
HISTORIC PRESERVATION STUDY

EXISTING DISTRICT (DESIGNATED 1966)

HISTORIC DISTRICT EXTENSION
(DESIGNATED 1988)

PROPOSED INDIVIDUAL LANDMARK

EXISTING INDIVIDUAL LANDMARK

THIRD AVENUE

FIFTH NATIONAL BANK
296-300 Third Avenue (aka 162 East 23rd Street)
Architect: James E. Ware
Date: 1874

T HE IMPOSING five-story building on the southwest corner of Third Avenue and East 23rd Street is an extraordinary survivor. This is one of the few bank buildings still standing in New York built before 1890. In the 1850s, the Italian Renaissance palazzo became the form for New York City's banks. A significant number of these buildings were erected in the Wall Street area. In the 1860s and 1870s, the basic form was adapted for Second Empire and Neo-Grec bank buildings. Although all but one of the early Wall Street banks have been demolished (the former Hanover Bank, now India House, stands on Hanover Square), several neighborhood banks from this era survive in New York City and Brooklyn. Among these are the former Kings County Savings Bank in Williamsburg, Brooklyn (1868), and the former Metropolitan Savings Bank on Third Avenue and East 7th Street (1867), both Second Empire buildings with mansard roofs, and this Neo-Grec style building.

The 23rd Street bank is massed in the manner of an Italianate palazzo with a rhythmic arrangement of horizontal windows, each with a three-dimensional pedimented enframement, and the entire structure is capped by a projecting cornice. Neo-Grec detailing is evident in the use of acroteria on the pediments of the central bay on Third Avenue and on the pedimented cornice. Other Neo-Grec features are the incised detailing found on the panels beneath the third-story windows (this survives at only one window), on some of the pilasters, and on the window lintels at the top floor. James E. Ware was a very prolific late-19th-century architect who designed this bank relatively early in his career. The building was originally planned to have the banking hall and offices on the first floor with flats above.[52] It is now a mixed-use commercial and residential structure.

---

52. The building permit filed with the Buildings Department (NB 547-74) is for a four-story building with a banking hall and three flats. Alteration permits issued as late as 1907 are for a four-story building. The present building is five stories tall. An alteration permit of 1911 (Alt. 1592-11) indicates a five-story building. Since the building appears as one unified structure and there is no indication, on the exterior, that the fifth floor was added at a later date, it is probable that the first-floor banking hall was originally a double-height space and was later divided into two separate floors. In 1911, the building still housed the Fifth National Bank. By 1922, the building was stores and offices with an assembly hall on the fifth floor.

NO. 300 THIRD AVENUE
Looking southwest

SCHEFFEL HALL
190 Third Avenue
Architect: unknown; new facade, Weber & Drosser
Date: unknown; new facade, 1894

IN THE LATE 19th century, the East Side, north and south of 14th Street, had a substantial German population. The presence of a German community in the area is evident in the design of Scheffel Hall, a beer hall and social center that catered to this ethnic group. The hall was named for Joseph Victor von Scheffel, a German balladeer known for his songs about fellowship and love. The exuberant German Renaissance building with its scrolled gable is actually a new facade placed on an older building in 1894 (the earlier building was probably a brick residence with a commercial ground floor). The Germanic theme was appropriate for the architecture of this ethnic social center. A history of Scheffel Hall, written early in the 20th century, suggests that architects Adam Weber and Hubert Drosser (both apparently German-born) worked from an idea of Carl Goerwitz, the establishment's first proprietor.[53]

Scheffel Hall was originally an L-shaped structure with two ornate facades and an exuberant interior with massive woodwork and murals based on themes from Scheffel's songs. The three-story frontage at 143 East 17th Street *(see pages 84, 85)* was demolished after being sold to the Greek Orthodox Church of St. John the Baptist. At the time that the building was converted into a restaurant, it was owned by Augustus Van Horn Stuyvesant, the last direct male descendant of Peter Stuyvesant; Goerwitz, who ran Scheffel Hall until 1909, appears to have been the lessee. The building later housed Allaire's, a reputed meeting place for German spies during World War I, and Joe King's Rathskeller. Since then it has housed a succession of other restaurants. The Landmarks Preservation Commission held a public hearing on the designation of this building in 1966, but no action was taken on the proposal.

---

53. *Scheffel-Halle,* undated brochure, n.p.

NO. 190 THIRD AVENUE
Originally Scheffel Hall

EAST 17TH STREET

141 EAST 17TH STREET
Architect: unknown; front extension, Jobst Hoffmann
Date: unknown; front extension, 1889

THIS BUILDING IS of interest for the flamboyant two-story front extension that was added in 1889 for owner/occupant Louise Bruner. This extension was planned with a store on the first floor and a residence above. The addition, faced in pressed metal, is somewhat Germanic in feeling with its six rectangular windows separated by attenuated colonnettes with bulbous bases. Above each window is a blind round arch. The cornice is supported by dwarf columns and is crowned by a parapet pierced by open roundels. In 1922, Henry Luce and Briton Hadden rented an office in the building. It was here that they came up with the idea of publishing the news magazine that became known as *Time*.[54]

NO. 141 EAST 17TH STREET, in 1992

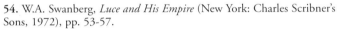

54. W.A. Swanberg, *Luce and His Empire* (New York: Charles Scribner's Sons, 1972), pp. 53-57.

NOS. 141 AND 143 EAST 17TH STREET
1938 photograph showing 1889 pressed-metal facing at No. 141 and the facade of part of Scheffel Hall at No. 143, which was demolished after being sold to its present owner, the Greek Orthodox Church of St. John the Baptist

No. 141 East 17th Street, in 1938

138   136   134

NOS. 134-138 EAST 16TH STREET
The middle house (No. 136) showing 1889 cast-iron facade
elements by Herter Brothers

134, 136, AND 138 EAST 16TH STREET
Architect: unknown; alteration to No. 136, Herter Brothers
Date: No. 134, 1846; Nos. 136 and 138,
     early 1850s; alteration to No. 136, 1889

NO. **134** IS a late example of a Greek Revival rowhouse that retains much of its original appearance. Of special note on this tall four-story and basement house is its entrance enframement. This contains typical Greek Revival brownstone pilasters and an unusual cornice. The Italianate residences at Nos. **136** and **138** were built somewhat later than No. 134.

The most unusual house of this trio, and one of the most extraordinary buildings in the Gramercy Park neighborhood, is No. **136**. The unique street facade probably dates from an alteration of 1889, when the architectural firm of Herter Brothers converted the single-family residence into five French flats.[55] This is an early conversion of a rowhouse into comfortable apartments and reflects the fact that the area between Union Square and Gramercy Park was becoming a popular section for middle-class apartment houses.[56] The brownstone front was updated by the addition of a series of cast-iron elements, including a free-standing Corinthian entrance portico capped by a pediment and window enframements with sawtooth detail and pyramidal bosses; all of the windows have triangular pediments except for those on the top floor, which are capped by ornamented blind fanlights. Also of note are the massive cornice, fine double doors, and cast-iron stoop railings and newel posts.

55. The Buildings Department permit (Alt. 299-89) describes the conversion to a five-family flat and the lowering of the areaway 18″ to be level with the basement floor. No mention is made of the new facade design, but since the facade changes were not structural, it was probably not necessary to list these changes on the application.

56. In the 19th century, many rowhouses became tenements, especially in areas south of 14th Street, but in most cases several families lived in an old rowhouse with little change made to the original building fabric.

NO. 136 EAST 16TH STREET
Entrance and window enframements

AD 1850

NO. 136 EAST 16TH STREET
Cast-iron window details

EAST 15TH STREET

Truman Moore

NO. 105 EAST 15TH STREET
and to the right at No. 109, the former Century Association Clubhouse,
a designated landmark

SWANNANOA
105 East 15th Street
Architect: Gilbert A. Schellinger
Date: 1898-1900

THE SWANNANOA is a 10-story Neo-Renaissance apartment building designed by a prolific designer of residential buildings whose name is generally associated with single-family rowhouses. The building was planned with 40 apartments, four on each floor. Its most imposing feature is the two-story base with granite pilasters and projecting portico supported by four granite columns. Above the portico are seven-story rounded bays, undoubtedly designed to provide residents with views toward nearby Union Square. The brick-faced upper floors are extensively ornamented with terra cotta, including foliate detail, cartouches, lion heads, and dolphins.

Truman Moore

NOS. 135 AND 137 EAST 15TH STREET
Architect unknown
Date: c. 1843 and early 1850s

THESE TWO four-story and basement rowhouses were erected in the initial stage of residential development in the Gramercy Park neighborhood. No. 135 is an imposing Greek Revival dwelling with a fine stone entrance enframement and exceptionally well-preserved wrought- and cast-iron railings; its cornice dates from later in the 19th century. No. 137 is a slightly later Italianate house that also retains a handsome stone entrance enframement and original ironwork.

Truman Moore

CONSOLIDATED EDISON COMPANY
No. 4 Irving Place, corner of 15th Street, looking southeast

CONSOLIDATED EDISON COMPANY
No. 4 Irving Place, 14th Street facade

Rockefeller, and in part in response to the "threat" posed by electricity. The new company established its headquarters at 4 Irving Place in the offices of the old Manhattan Gas Light Company. This was a handsome Italianate brownstone building erected for the company's use in 1854. The Consolidated Gas Company continued to grow in the late 19th century, eventually allying itself with various electrical companies, notably the New York Edison Company. The firm outgrew its headquarters building and began an expansion project that lasted for almost 20 years. Major buildings were erected on virtually the entire block bounded by East 14th and 15th streets, Irving Place, and Third Avenue.

The expansion began in 1910, when Consolidated Gas decided to build a new 12-story headquarters on Irving Place and 15th Street. The prominent architect Henry Hardenbergh, best-known for such buildings as the Dakota Apartments, Plaza Hotel, and Hotel Martinique, was commissioned to design the new structure. Since the company did not wish to disturb the ongoing work of the office, construction was planned in two sections. A 12-story building was erected at the rear of the lot, behind the old office. This was completed in 1911, the offices were moved, and the old headquarters building on the corner demolished. By this time, however, the firm had decided that a 12-story building would be inadequate. More land was purchased to the east, and Hardenbergh was requested to design an 18-story building for the entire site. There was no problem in constructing the structures for the east and west sides of the lot, but the original 12-story central section did not have a structural system that could support extra floors. The solution was to

CONSOLIDATED GAS COMPANY
　　　(now Consolidated Edison Company)
4 Irving Place
Architect: Henry Hardenbergh; additions, Warren &
　　　Wetmore and Thomas E. Murray, Inc.
Date: 1910-14; additions, 1926-29

THE CONSOLIDATED GAS COMPANY was formed in 1884 with the merger of six of the city's independent gas companies.[57] This merger took place, in part, as a response to the threat created by the formation of the Equitable Gas Light Company, backed by William

57. For a history of New York's gas companies as seen from the viewpoint of the companies themselves, see Frederick L. Collins, *Consolidated Gas Company of New York: A History* (New York: Consolidated Gas Company, 1934). The company was renamed Consolidated Edison in 1936.

build the end wings and then construct girders between them and suspend the additional stories.[58] As completed in 1914, the Consolidated Gas Company's building was a Renaissance Revival skyscraper clad in limestone with an Ionic entrance portico and enormous cornice crowned by acroteria.

With the increasing use of electricity, Consolidated grew rapidly and on April 10, 1926, announced plans for a tower to be erected on the site of the old Academy of Music on the corner of 14th Street and Irving Place.[59] The architectural firm of Warren & Wetmore designed the new tower in conjunction with the engineering firm of Thomas E. Murray, Inc. Although Warren & Wetmore is best known for its work on Grand Central Terminal and other imposing early-20th-century Beaux-Arts monuments, during the 1920s the firm designed a significant number of important skyscrapers, including the Heckscher Building and Aeolian Building, both on Fifth Avenue, the New York Central Building on Park Avenue, and this prominent office tower on 14th Street.

Much of the 14th Street elevation of the new building was designed to copy Hardenbergh's original structure. However, for the corner, Warren & Wetmore designed a 26-story tower that would be a prominent landmark as it rose above the low buildings of its neighborhood and would be a visible symbol of the utility company. The tower is faced with limestone and has a three-story Doric colonnade at the base. The tall shaft is set back from the colonnade and rises uninterrupted 21 stories to a modest cornice, above which are four clockfaces and four corner urns. Near the top, the tower sets back slightly and takes the form of a temple capped by a pyramidal roof that is crowned by a 38-foot-high bronze lantern. This tower was planned to be dramatically lighted at night, advertising the wonders of the electricity that the company sold. Known as the "Tower of Light," this was a memorial to the company's employees who had died in World War I. The building was well-received upon completion; an editorial published in *The Architect* commented that "the new tower-building designed by Warren and Wetmore...is, to our mind, a building of unusual merit and distinction."[60] Since it was built for the country's leading utility company, the tower also had an influence on the design of electric-company buildings in other cities; for example, John Russell Pope's Cincinnati Gas & Electric Company Building (1930) is a light-colored stone building with a Doric base on which sits a setback tower crowned by a pyramidal roof. Lighted at night, the Con Edison tower is now a potent symbol of the corporation.

In 1928, Consolidated Gas again expanded, purchasing the old Tammany Hall building on 14th Street.[61] Warren & Wetmore's addition, built in 1928-29, simply extends the earlier 14th Street elevation.

Truman Moore

CONSOLIDATED EDISON COMPANY
No. 4 Irving Place, tower at corner of 14th Street

58. "An Innovation in Construction Methods," *Real Estate Record and Builders Guide 93* (March 14, 1914), p. 481.

59. "Academy of Music Ending its Career," *New York Times,* April 11, 1926, Sec. XI, p. 2.

60. "Editorially Speaking," *The Architect 12* (August 1929), pp. 495-96, 513-31; also see, "Towering Office Building to Replace Academy of Music," *Real Estate Record and Builders Guide 117* (April 10, 1926), p. 7; "Consolidated Gas Company's Building, New York City," *Architecture and Building 60* (December 1928), p. 376.

61. "Wigwam Sold Again at $100,000 Profit," *New York Times,* January 2, 1928, p. 2. Tammany had sold this building to a real-estate syndicate in December 1927 and had begun construction of its new headquarters on the corner of 17th Street and Union Square East. According to the *Times,* Consolidated Gas was afraid that the syndicate would build a skyscraper on the site that would overshadow its new tower.

91

AUDEN, W. H., in 1939................................George Washington Hotel,
Poet   23 Lexington Avenue

AXELROD, GEORGE..71 Irving Place
Writer

BARA, THEDA..132 East 19th Street
Actress

BEAUX, CECILIA..19 Gramercy Park South
Painter

BEMELMANS, LUDWIG ....19 Gramercy Park South
Illustrator and writer

BIGELOW, JOHN..21 Gramercy Park South
Statesman

CAMPBELL, MRS. PATRICK ....132 East 19th Street
Actress

CHANLER, ROBERT ....147/9 East 19th Street
Painter

CRANE, HART, site of home, in 1917 ....44 Gramercy Park North
Poet

CRANE, STEPHEN, site of home, in 1893 ....145 East 23rd Street
Writer

DE WOLFE, ELSIE /ELISABETH (Bessie) MARBURY ....49 Irving Place
Interior designer/companion and literary agent

EDISON, THOMAS ALVA, site of home ....24 Gramercy Park South
Inventor

FISH, STUYVESANT..20 Gramercy Park South
Businessman

FRENCH, DANIEL CHESTER ....36 Gramercy Park East
Sculptor

GILDER, RICHARD WATSON.............................24 Gramercy Park South
Editor

HERTS & TALLANT ....113 East 19th Street
Architects

HEWITT, EDWARD...48 Gramercy Park North
Inventor

HOMER, WINSLOW, home in 1859 & 1861 ....128 East 16th Street
Painter

IRVING, WASHINGTON ....41 East 21st Street
site where he lived and worked while in New York
(home of his nephew, John Treat Irving)
Writer, diplomat, and historian

IVES, CHARLES, site of home ....120 East 22nd Street
Composer

KENNEDY, JOHN F. ....Gramercy Park Hotel, 2 Lexington Avenue
Politician and 35th U.S. President

KENNEDY, JOSEPH P. ....Gramercy Park Hotel, 2 Lexington Avenue
Businessman and diplomat

McCARTHY, MARY ....Gramercy Park Hotel, 2 Lexington Avenue
Writer

NATIONAL CONSERVATORY OF MUSIC OF AMERICA, site of ....
....126/8 East 17th Street
Where Antonin Dvorak and
Victor Herbert taught; Dvorak was also the Director

PERELMAN, S. J. ....Gramercy Park Hotel, 2 Lexington Avenue
Writer

PHELPS STOKES, ISAAC NEWTON, site of home...... 118 East 22nd Street
Architect and historian

RINGLING, JOHN ....36 Gramercy Park East
Circus impresario

SAINT-GAUDENS, AUGUSTUS, site of home ....304 Third Avenue
Sculptor   site of studio, 145 Fourth Avenue

SONNENBERG, BENJAMIN.................................19 Gramercy Park South
Publicist

STEINBECK, JOHN, home in 1925 ....38 Gramercy Park East
Writer

STEVENS, WALLACE, site of home .... 124 East 24th Street
Poet

STRONG, GEORGE TEMPLETON, site of home ....Gramercy Park Hotel
Diarist and patron of the arts   Addition, 52 Gramercy Park North

TARBELL, IDA ....120 East 19th Street
Writer and newspaperwoman

TARKINGTON, BOOTH ....26 Gramercy Park South
Writer

THOMAS, NORMAN ....71 Irving Place
Politician and Socialist

TIME MAGAZINE, birthplace of ....141 East 17th Street
Begun by Henry Luce and Briton Hadden

WEST, NATHANAEL ....Hotel Kenmore, 145 East 23rd Street
Writer

WHARTON, EDITH ....14 West 23rd Street
Writer

WILDE, OSCAR ....47 Irving Place
Writer and playwright

WILSON, EDMUND ....Gramercy Park Hotel, 2 Lexington Avenue
Writer

Many people have helped and encouraged our Historic Preservation Committee in this project and we would like to express our appreciation and gratitude to them:

Our thanks for editorial and research assistance:
EDITH CHARLTON, ETHYL CHURCHILL, MARION CLEAVER, JOHN M. COLLINS, Community Board Six, Manhattan: Parks and Landmarks Committee, ROBERT CRANE, SUZANNE DAVIS, ROBERT DURKIN, FRANCES EBERHART, ANDREW GENN, LINDA GILLIES, ELLIOTT M. GLASS, CHRISTABEL GOUGH, MARION GREENWOOD, ALEXANDRA C. HOWARD, O. ALDON JAMES, OLIVER JOHNSTON, EDWARD S. KIRKLAND, ANDREW KNER, CAROL KNER, Landmarks Preservation Commission, JULIE LASKY, MARGARET MOORE, W. CARLYLE MORRIS, Historic Districts Council: Certificate of Appropriateness Committee, PEG MULLIGAN, TOM O'BRIEN, MICHAEL OSHEOWITZ, GARY PAPUSH, SUSAN POWERS, TIM SCANLON, RICHARD SNIBBE, MELISSA SUTPHEN, SUSAN TUNICK, REX WASSERMANN, and ANTHONY C. WOOD.

Our thanks for financial assistance:
The Vincent Astor Foundation, Chase Manhattan Bank, FREDERICK GORREE, Edwin Gould Foundation, ALEXANDRA C. HOWARD, The J. M. Kaplan Fund, Joyce Mertz-Gilmore Foundation, ASHER LANS, Mr. & Mrs. THOMAS MAHERAS, DUANE MICHALS, Mr. & Mrs. PETER RYAN, JACK TAYLOR, TESNA (The Eighteenth Street Neighborhood Alliance), and TRESSA (The Residents of East Seventeenth Street Association).

Our thanks for the insightful photography:
THE REVEREND STEPHEN GARMEY, FREDERICK GORREE, TRUMAN MOORE, BARRY PRIBULA, and TODD WEINSTEIN.

Our thanks for the book's computer assistance:
VALERIE CASTLEMAN and DEBBIE WAGNER.

Gramercy Neighborhood Associates, Inc., Historic Preservation Committee:
JAMES D. DOUGHERTY, THE REVEREND STEPHEN GARMEY, PETER RYAN, JACK TAYLOR, NANCY ZUGER, **and FREDERICK GORREE, Chairman and Book Director/Producer. New York, 1996**

GNA Archives

GRAMERCY PARK (LOWER LEFT CORNER) IN 1907
Neighborhood view taken from the Metropolitan Life Insurance Company Tower,
looking southwest